Ballet Studio

URE SMITH

Sydney · Auckland · London · New York

Ballet Studio
An Inside View

By Anne Woolliams · Photographs by Andreas Heumann

First published in English 1978 by
Mereweather Press, Inc.
598 Madison Avenue
New York, N.Y. 10022 U.S.A.

Published in Australia 1978 by
Ure Smith
a division of Paul Hamlyn Pty Limited
176 South Creek Road, Dee Why West, Australia 2099

Text © Copyright Anne Woolliams 1978

Photographs © Copyright Andreas Heumann 1973, 1978
All photographs were taken with a Leicaflex

Designed by Gael Towey Dillon
Typeset by American Book-Stratford Press
Printed in Hong Kong

National Library of Australia Cataloguing-in-Publication
Number and ISBN 0 7254 0437 X

This book was first published in 1973
in German as BALLETTSAAL

Table of Contents

Preface

Walking across the ballet studio in Stuttgart, Anne Woolliams carefully gripped the leg of one of her dancers and lifted it gently through an arch into the thrust forward position of *développé*. To the dancer she explained in a voice both gentle and audible to all the other dancers, "*Développé,* is not about how high the leg goes but rather how it gets to where it is going. It's the shape, not the elevation, which matters most. Now why don't you try it again with that in mind." It wasn't a command, it was an invitation.

That incident took place in 1970 in one of the airy studios in the Staatstheatre where John Cranko and Anne Woolliams molded what was to become one of the great dance companies of our time. It was the first time that I had met her and watched her at work, but not the first time I had seen her. Years before, as a starry-eyed balletomane, I'd unknowingly watched her in the ballet sequences in "The Red Shoes," an anonymous pair of point shoes in the Corps. Here in the ballet studio, the anonymity disappeared, and she became a marvellous blend of discipline and understanding, strength and inspiration.

In ballet studios around the world, in Stockholm where she mounted "Eugene Onegin" for the Royal Swedish Ballet, in Melbourne as Artistic Director of the Australian Ballet before taking on her current post as Dean of Dance at the Victorian College of the Arts, on the amphitheater stage of the Garden State Arts Center in New Jersey, Anne Woolliams always brought something very special to the dancers she served and who in turn served her. She gave them the gift of understanding the difference between technique and art and taught them how to use the first to achieve the second. And she gave them love at the moments when it mattered most, stern reprimands when occasion demanded.

Those ballet studios where Anne Woolliams has taught and rehearsed live vividly in the memory of the dancers who were lucky enough to work with her. BALLET STUDIO is a typically unselfish effort to extend that circle and to make the art of ballet accessible to an even wider audience.

Peter J. Rosenwald
Dance Critic for *The Wall Street Journal*

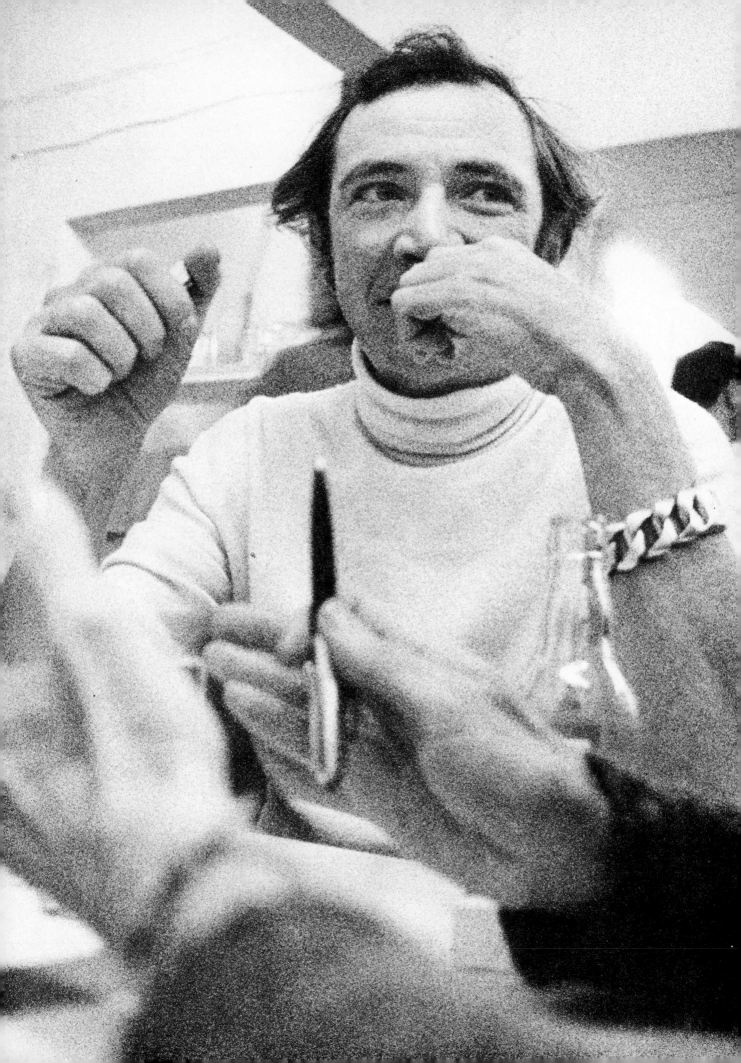

Foreword

'What a pity she is only a body dancer.' This blistering condemnation of a fellow dancer came from the lips of a member of the Royal Danish Ballet. Yet it expresses in a nutshell everything about dance. What was meant was that although the dancer in question had all the correct physical requirements to be a dancer, there was no artist in that 'body-machine' to express anything, therefore one was left entirely indifferent to its pyrotechnics.

Great teachers in ballet history (how many there were and how few are remembered!) have always been concerned not only with the physical discipline but also with the developing mind and imagination within the body, bringing the flesh and the spirit into union.

Although Miss Woolliams has many practical things to say, it is her method of achieving this union which makes her book so valuable.

There are legions of books which illustrate the correct positions and movements in dance, but as far as I know this is the only one which attempts to elucidate the process from teacher to pupil, the process of not only *what* to do, but *how* to do it and how to *think* it. Very often it is not the movement itself, but the *wish* behind the movement which is important. The dancer must be an artist who can control his highly specialized machine as he wishes, and not the reverse! What Miss Woolliams has to say is extremely personal, which is as it should be. There is no one infallible way to heaven. Dogmatic methods taught *one* way lead to conveyor-belt results. Although a school must have a unified way of teaching to avoid complete confusion in its pupils there must be enough freedom to establish the teacher-pupil relationship which is vital, and I do mean each individual pupil.

Seeing is believing (or disbelieving), and the extreme difficulty of this book is describing in words what in fact are visual happenings. Both Miss Woolliams and I had the extreme luck and joy to study with Vera Volkova, a humble woman whose quiet words remain with us to this day. Today Miss Woolliams' teaching has been of inestimable value to the Stuttgart Ballet. She is to be felt everywhere, from our prima-ballerina to our kindergarten.

I am reminded of the old Russian proverb 'One word of truth is of more weight than the rest of the world.' If we are able to transmit this word to but a few of our pupils, the efforts of the many people who have helped to make the Stuttgart Ballet School possible will have been justified.

John Cranko
1973

Introduction

Since the German publication of this book, John Cranko has died. Full of plans for future seasons, he was suddenly and prematurely taken from us. Though the amputation and shock need time to heal, the body of the company, through its youth and vitality, remains healthy. The repertoire John left and the company he built is based on solid foundations, for he was a director of depth. Although perhaps much appeared to rest upon the considerable personality of the man and the magnetic qualities of his creative genius this was a superficial impression, for he had in fact given more than just his presence and his ballets to Stuttgart. There existed something greater within Cranko than a mere ego projecting only his own creations, and his love endures.

When Walter Erich Schäfer engaged John Cranko to be ballet master in Stuttgart, he provided fertile ground for an embryo company and over the years, in his wisdom, protected both John and his group of dancers from storm and drought. Cranko activated the growth and, by his great belief in the impossible, 'fed' his dancers and inspired all who worked with him. He was never condescending and seldom severely authoritative, but he expected much. He truly believed in the dignity of the individual and therefore, by assuming his company and colleagues would behave as super cultivated and sensitive artists, received in return every effort by each person to be just this. One learned especially to estimate things of real value, and the cruelties of the bogus fell into perspective.

The Stuttgart Ballet owes its existence to John.

Although the 'Ballettsaal' of this book is to be found in reality on the second floor of the Württembergisches Staatstheater, it nevertheless exists, with small variations, all over the world. From the sacred studios of Paris, Leningrad, Copenhagen and Milan, to the huge windowless basement of the Lincoln Center in New York; from the famous Monte Carlo cellar, where one wonders how any lifted dancer managed to avoid the pipes and girders criss-crossing the ceiling, to the airy halls of modern ballet schools, all have heard the same music, seen the same disappointments and success, and experienced the strange still hours of silence when the dancers are absent.

Four walls and a wooden floor, a *barre*, a mirror and a piano do not alone make a ballet studio, only the creativity within can legitimize this room; and in turn, only a creative choreographer, plus a master-mind to provide and organize the participants, can produce this activity. In Stuttgart Cranko and Schäfer respectively filled these roles.

Having had two simultaneous functions in this complex which brought me into daily contact with both school and company, I became very aware of the rebirth necessary to students when transferring from the former to the latter. The aim of so many schools is merely to place their students into companies. What happens after this is outside their control, and though they naturally wish for the further success of their products, the immediate goal is reached. Sometimes students will find themselves completely lost and unprepared for the tacit hierarchy existing in companies. They will miss the admiration of junior members of their late school and will feel frustrated when the technical stunts for which they have been striving are a matter of small interest to the company dancers. It is this gap I would like to bridge, and so this book is written mainly for young people, students and *corps de ballet* members and, perhaps as a refresher, for the teachers helping these young artists.

11

It was originally intended that this book should be illustrated with photographs directly relating to the text: Dancers in performance, children training, the right way and the wrong. However, it was rescued from this prosaic fate by the arrival of Andreas Heumann. Having no experience of ballet, his eye was pure and unerringly direct. Confronted by the illusion laid naked, he fell in love with the essence. His photos reveal a lot that is unsaid and are, therefore, the best possible substitute for the inadequacies of the word.

Heumann's pictures need no explanation, and their mood is what this book is about.

All the photographs were made in Stuttgart and show the company and school rehearsing and in class. No dancers are named, as it is especially the working atmosphere of the ballet studio which creates a homogenous whole, as opposed to the performance of individuals. I would like to express my gratitude and affection to all members of the company and school who, by their concentration and diligence, unknowingly made these illustrations possible.

Anne Woolliams
1978

1. Ballet as a Profession

At the risk of offending many well-intentioned, loving and self-sacrificing ladies, I still believe Noel Coward's advice to Mrs. Worthington holds good for most ballet mothers. It also applies to those who launch their daughters in a ballet school with the words 'of course her father doesn't want her to take it up *seriously,* but she *does* so enjoy dancing to the radio.' Whereas some fathers, at the first intelligent utterance of their young, see their sons as Prime Ministers or Presidents, even more mothers see paths of glory lined with sighing admirers stretching before their daughters. They will become beings elevated above the vacuum cleaner and the washing machine; a life of fame, glamour, riches and travel awaits them. They will become in fact nothing less than prima ballerinas. How sad is often the lot of these idolized children. When Mary at the age of twelve tips the scales at nine stone, mother still does not see the light and Mary is already brainwashed into believing her goal can only be the great theatres of the world. I believe no other profession exists that can magnetize more acolytes at the age of ten, or reject more discards at the age of twenty. The answer is 'don't put your daughter on the stage.' If the stage wants her, it will find her. Those who are made for the ballet are predestined, and will find their course against all odds, like eels crossing dry land to reach the river of whose whereabouts only instinct can tell them. These will be the good dancers, the professionals, the enduring dancers. These will know that, metaphorically, one crosses the dry land on one's stomach to get there; and when one is there, one has to swim to survive and avoid all nets and hooks to remain in the stream. Ballet is not a profession for the weak, the vacillating or the lazy. Nor is it a career for the arrogant, the insensitive or the uncouth.

Dancing is for everyone. Ballet as a profession is for the very few.

The gulf between the two is enormous and to prevent a plunge into its abyss, the existence of this chasm should be understood. To be more explicit, no child should be prevented from learning to dance. On the contrary, they should be urged to do so. Many races still 'dance' as a part of life, and for the lucky children belonging to these countries there is no problem. Others live where dancing schools are plentiful and emancipated parents encourage their children to learn. As mechanized living takes over, however, physical activity declines, and while poor little rich children have to be driven to their classes in limousines, costing time and trouble, the even less privileged sit at home watching television. Nevertheless, dancing prevails, and even the most scientifically developed communities still shuffle about to music when engaged in social gathering. Now, however, comes the gulf. Professional ballet is as far removed from social dancing as *marons glacés* from conkers.

The real classical ballet dancer is a very rare bird and emerges only when nearly all the following circumstances combine. He or she must possess physical beauty. The anatomy and constitution must comply with classical ballet tenets. He or she must be endowed with talent, intelligence, willpower and dedication; a strong sense of rhythm, co-ordination and energy, good health, good humour, and all the other attributes associated with grace and charm. He or she must have the opportunity to start learning dancing at no later than twelve years of age for a girl, or fourteen for a boy (preferably four years earlier for both), and the good fortune of a knowledgeable and inspiring teacher to guide him. Ideally, he or she should be exposed to the work of first-class dancers, choreographers and musicians from an early age, and be in contact with such people during the formative period of adolescence. Of course there are paragons like this singing in the wilderness, but to fulfill all possibilities this rare creature should also have the added bonus to be seen at the right time, in the right place, by the right person. Only those who have been found can be cherished, and then everything must be done to retain their song and the colours of their plumage.

Now let us suppose some such mortal evolves in a family unconnected with the stage. What can the parents expect for the child and what advantages can a future in a ballet company offer over a 'normal' job? Perhaps the biggest is fulfillment. Those who find a job doing the things they love and do best are not working to exist, nor yet existing to work: they are in harmony with themselves, and this is a very great advantage indeed. A successful dancer can expect to travel widely and will have opportunities to meet not only the people of many lands, but also the interesting, the famous and the bizarre. The world, with all its strata of society, opens itself sooner to artists than to other mortals. Probably because the artists reflect life in which each individual can identify himself, they are welcomed as an embodiment of the average man's personal escape wish. Dancers are nearly always tolerant and without cant, they have usually no axe to grind and therefore do not endanger the defensive barriers which groups of people build around their societies. Social discrimination is abhorrent to artists; in a ballet company, a small group of hard-working people, often drawn from many nationalities and from every conceivable background, an immensely powerful common bond is forged by merely working together. Many people in the world of ballet speak two or three languages, frequently not because of education, but because the facilities for learning them are all to hand. This often helps to do away with inhibitions and makes contact with other people more direct and mutually productive. Another advantage is that it does make people happy to bring pleasure to others. And this is what dancers can do. It may be argued that the boy selling ice-cream or a pretty girl smiling also brings pleasure, but the real artist can touch deeper chords within people and enrich and strengthen that place we all have inside us for something mystic and spiritual in our humdrum lives. In short, a dancer has every opportunity for becoming a real person.

If the parents want more concrete assurance that their child will be materially equipped for the future, one can only repeat that any career is a gamble and that success in the ballet is neither more nor less dependent upon good luck and uncontrollable events than any other. Certainly the very famous can earn considerable sums of money and in isolated cases may be compared to the great stars of opera, stage and film, but generally it has to be admitted that a dancer's salary is in no way commensurate with the length and expense of training and the shortness of the career. All this is changing slowly. State theatres supporting a ballet are gradually increasing salaries and providing adequate security and pensions as the accepted norm, but in general the future of dancers can be precarious.

In Germany, where conditions for theatre artists are now probably better than in any other Western European country, it is still a disgrace that the minimum salary for a young person entering the *corps de ballet* after ten years' training and very competitive auditioning, is dependent upon the size of the orchestra—the yardstick by which German State theatres are graded—and is in any case well below the lowest salary for members of the opera chorus. The discrepancy remains throughout a dancer's career: even as first soloist, dancers cannot command salaries equivalent to those of their colleagues in opera. This attitude of indifference to the worth of dancers

seems to be inconsistent with the present enthusiasm for diplomatic exchange of ballet companies and the use of 'dance' as a cultural prestige symbol. The trained body of a dancer is perhaps the most specialized and perfected instrument used in any of the arts, but because performance is entirely dependent upon strenuous physical exertion it cannot function at top level for as long as the instruments of artists in other branches of the theatre, thus reducing the span of a professional career.

Undoubtedly this is a contributing factor to the shortage of boys seriously taking up ballet as a career in the Western world, and though I understand the misgivings of parents, I do feel that in spite of this a boy should be given the chance to make his future in the ballet if this is what he desires. Parents should understand that (provided school lessons are not forfeited) a boy receiving a daily dance class until he is sixteen cannot possibly be endangering any future career, but can be building an athletic body and making the chances of success in the ballet, should he decide to become a professional, infinitely more probable. A competent male dancer will usually have no trouble finding engagements and can, on average, expect to earn a steadily increasing salary from eighteen or nineteen years of age until forty, or, if he is a character dancer, even longer. I am often asked, what happens then? At forty a man should be entering into the most productive and successful era of his life, whereas the dancer's career is just finishing. This is not as bad as it sounds. At forty he may come to the end of his 'active' dancing days, but it is precisely then that all he has learnt in his long apprenticeship can be put to use. Apprenticeship, one may ask, for what? I can only repeat: for becoming a person. 'This is no material assurance,' says the father, and he is right. It depends entirely upon what a man needs from life and upon what he holds most valuable. As an active performer a man can support himself and a family in reasonable comfort for about twenty years, or, if he takes part in films or becomes famous, he may provide above-average comfort. After this, should he not qualify for any retirement scheme, there are several avenues still open to him.

CHOREOGRAPHER. To be successful, he should have started creating or arranging ballets during his dancing career. It is a method of earning a living that can be neither taught nor learnt and is almost totally dependent upon musicality, which is essential, and a balanced amalgam of inherent talents. It is a grave misconception to think that any imaginative mortal with the courage and drive to express his ideas can one day just start to arrange ballets. Before the creative talent of a choreographer can become productive he must first be completely familiar with the vocabulary of classic and/or contemporary dancing and possess a knowledge of, or instinctive feeling for, folklore. He must also be sufficiently mature to deal with a company of dancers called together at a specific time, for a specific purpose, and all waiting for his instant inspiration to feed their performing ambitions. To some extent a choreographer is always dependent on collaborators and interpreters, for these people can make a good ballet better or sometimes camouflage the faults if it is bad. It will be seen that a lot of hard work and craftsmanship go into the birth of a ballet and that many years of apprenticeship, usually as a dancer, go into the making of a choreographer.

BALLET MASTER AND/OR TEACHER. For this it is even more essential that a man should have had a complete ballet training and have spent many years as a member of a dance company. Only personal experience can equip a person to deal

with the multitudinous problems and crises that occur when working at the junction point between choreographer, dancer, conductor, wardrobe and administration. A good ballet master should have the respect of his company, be endowed with patience and a good eye, be firm and fair, and if possible, able to preserve life in the ballets he rehearses after the burning excitement of creation has worn off a new work and the choreographer is pregnant with his next ballet.

For a teacher this theatre experience is not quite so essential, though it is an advantage, especially when teaching professionals or advanced students. However, a well-trained boy or girl, after only a few years in the theatre can, if he or she is pedagogically gifted, make a long and successful career as a teacher.

CRITIC. It is not fair to say that dancers are either illiterate or uneducated. In fact, many of them are very well read and the possessors of healthy and analytical minds which should well equip them to pass judgement on ballets. However, because dancers in general retain an unquenchable involvement with the physical, as opposed to the intellectual, happenings on the stage, they could lack objectivity as critics. It is also doubtful if this can be legitimately included as a career for dancers, as the business of earning a living by writing is dependent upon full-time journalism and/or a real literary gift.

Many other jobs in theatres are open to dancers, from stage management to administration and from production to design. Dancers usually have a strong visual sense and sometimes find themselves in these latter branches of art. Also, because of the broad basis of experience, usually acquired while touring in foreign countries and by meeting others in so many walks of life, theatre people are often able to absorb new ideas and adapt easily to other occupations.

Nearly all the previously mentioned jobs are also available to women, though here the problem of a later career is not so acute as the majority of girls will marry, perhaps comparatively late, between twenty-five and thirty-five, and will make healthy and youthful mothers.

Of course not all trained dancers enter ballet companies, nor wish to. Because the supply is infinitely larger than the demand, many companies have become choosy, accepting only applicants of exceptional talent, or from the cream of their own schools. This has two advantages. First, the standard of the average dancer in a ballet company has risen enormously, and secondly, it makes available well trained and gifted artists to other branches of the theatre and films. Many join opera ballet companies or television groups or dance in musicals on the commercial stage. In the United States the standard of dancing in shows is very high and this may be attributed to several factors. Some of the best choreographers in the world work on Broadway and thereby attract talent. The individual competition for each dancer is enormous and, though perhaps too cut-throat, it is definitely stimulating; on top of this, the profession is envied and respected. This is also true in Russia where artists are particularly cherished and equally respected whether they are working in their beloved ballet, circus, music hall or ethnic dance groups. Particularly in the Eastern European countries male dancers are esteemed no less than other performing artists such as musicians, singers and actors. Though the Western world occasionally seems still to be wallowing in the aftermath of the decadent nineteenth century, where the male dancer was reduced to a secondary role in ballet, more and more modern choreog-

raphers are creating for men, often using them as the central figures and at last returning to ballet the excitement and vigour that has so long been lacking. In nearly all ethnic dancing it is the men who play the dominant role, performing virtuoso steps and making the more spectacular display. With their greater muscular strength this is also possible in ballet and it is evident in the Soviet companies.

While all dancers cannot be termed paragons of virtue, the popular misconceptions concerning their lives are multitudinous. The office worker jogging to his desk in the nine o'clock rush hour believes a dancer is still sleeping off the effects of the previous night's party; he certainly does not imagine this glamorous being also jogging in the remnants of this same rush hour to his daily ten o'clock class. A salesgirl probably believes that after every performance the ballerina, weighed down with orchids and Chanel No. 5, is picked up in an Alfa Romeo and escorted to romantic assignments, while in fact she is most likely washing her tights and having a quick boiled egg before going to bed. All this belief in *la vie dorée* only adds to the glamour of ballet and indirectly benefits the dancer. Also it is not my intention to paint the full and colourful life of dancers a drab grey, but these very conscientious and hard working individuals do sometimes suffer unnecessarily from the misunderstanding of people 'outside' the ballet. When, for instance, landladies slam the door on prospective tenants with 'We don't want no theatricals 'ere',' the dancer's amazement is justified. He is usually too busy to be political, too tired to be noisy, too disciplined to make trouble and too loving to be promiscuous. Where other people seek sensation because of lack of drama in their lives, dancers live in an atmosphere of highly charged back-stage tension and their private lives even out in reverse by being often domestic and above all faithful.

I think it is true to say that ballet is more a vocation than a profession and few dancers are embarked upon the career with thoughts of financial gain. It is however not without compensations. Dance in our time has risen rapidly to become an explosive art form and being part of this dynamic force is, for young people, both exciting and rewarding.

2. Teaching

Imparting a knowledge of dancing to the young is similar to placing a grain of sand inside the shell of an oyster. Only when one knows the trick of opening this creature without causing damage, can one then hope for a cultured pearl as the result; unless of course that great rarity, a natural pearl, is already within. Children differ only in that whereas an oyster, unattended, will layer by layer slowly cover the seed with mother of pearl, young people must be helped daily to do this, and even then it is possible that the seed has been sown in a cockle.

Much has been written on the subject of ballet technique, but like all performing arts, it cannot be learned from books alone. Teachers can be helped on points about which they are unsure, and all should have a knowledge of the different methods of training, past and present, which are recorded in libraries, but only a relationship of mutual trust and respect between pupil and instructor can produce satisfactory results. This work takes place in the ballet studio.

I am personally rather sceptical of an 'applied psychology' approach to children and much prefer a natural direct manner, using common sense in dealing with their problems. However, one cannot deny that all teaching—and ballet is no exception—depends largely on the personality of the instructor. This means that the same individual can be bridge or stumbling block to different children, which is already a psychological factor. An inspired or conscientious teacher will recognize this, and while trying to remain fair and without prejudice or favourites, will endeavour to give each child personal care in the manner in which it will be most beneficial. Nevertheless, this should not become a conscious exercise in psychiatry.

There are many systems for teaching classical ballet. The purpose of this book is not to discuss the pros and cons of each method, but rather to show the need for having some system by which children who hope to become professional dancers should be taught. I believe that yearly examinations are an incentive for children and place a goal within their sight which gives the perfecting of the steps they are learning more urgency. It also gives teachers a consistent method to follow, which is impossible where classes are unsystematic.

Naturally, where more than two teachers are working together it is essential that a unified system is taught or children may receive contradictory corrections, and, without intent, the work of one instructor may be undermined by another. To arrive at a standardized approach, without courting the dangers of a dictatorial system, I believe the following are the minimum essentials for a framework to organized teaching:

1. classes divided into yearly grades
2. a given number of steps, carefully chosen for the right progression, to be learnt and mastered each year
3. consistent terminology
4. complete unanimity between teachers concerning analytical details of all steps

Thus, a child passing into the next class with perhaps a new teacher, will not be required to 'undo' half the previous year's work but will be able to add bricks to the existing foundation, building towards the final structure with planned precision.

Many instructors feel that by adhering to a rigid syllabus their classes will lose spontaneity, or that their own individual approach will stifle. There is, I agree, a risk

that a teacher confined to an inflexible plan may become unimaginative and impersonal and that the resulting products will be dulled, but any teacher of intelligence must be aware of the need for an organized approach to his work, and a teacher of character will find the actual imparting and correcting of all the steps still remains his personal challenge, and the successes his reward.

To avoid conflict, teachers working together in large schools should always discuss and agree upon the fundamentals that must be insisted upon and the degree of liberty that may be permitted. They will thus ensure (a) that the students receive the best possible preparation for the stage, and (b) that the teachers themselves understand what is being done in their colleagues' classes so that the minimum of overlapping, contradiction and jealousy occurs.

How much individual freedom should be allowed to instructors gives rise to interesting debate. No one can deny that the Russians have arrived at a formula for producing strong and beautiful dancers perhaps unequalled in the world today, but though a perfectly functioning body is an enormous asset to a dancer, I personally believe it should never be developed at the cost of a student's independence. The sparks of rebellion shown by some children often denote a free spirit and, sometimes, a creative talent cutting its teeth. Therefore, where a teacher is forced to subdue a class into uniform acquiescence, children of this individualistic kind will not be tolerated and in this way potential artists may well be lost or destroyed. I find it hard to believe that the present poverty of Russian choreography can be caused by a 'national' lack of creative imagination; and if some other explanation is sought, could not the rigidity of the Soviet Ballet school system be a contributory factor? Although compromise is usually a feeble conclusion at which to arrive, in this case a middle course is essential. On the one hand it has to be remembered that children are being taught to be artists and not machines, and, on the other, that any teaching system must incorporate firm control as well as freedom. This control entails gentle discipline, ensuring that regular daily exercises are performed, building technique and physique. The freedom is necessary for young people to mature as artists, eventually to be spiritually released by complete control of physical movement, which is the dancer's vocabulary. This may seem confused and contradictory, but the creation of a dancer is far from simple. In spite of this, it probably does no harm for teachers to remember that ultimate success may depend more upon the talent of the child than upon educational theorizing.

Sometimes a teacher's ambition will lead to the concoction of a child prodigy, capable of executing to perfection difficult steps beyond the required standard for his or her age and grade but with little regard for the need for 'slow cooking'. All too many students appear an appetizing brown outside but inside are still raw. This is usually the result of unsystematic training and results in a short-lived career for the dancer.

I realize that in many small private schools the facilities for following some of the well-known methods are not available. Should this be the case, the teacher must either work out for himself the rate of progress to be expected from his pupils and the order in which the steps should be graded according to the local needs or, with the help of an experienced teacher or association, adapt an already existing method. It is important, however, that an instructor should believe in the method he is employing. It is utterly useless to force pedagogic laws on young teachers and expect them to be transferred to the pupils. Most teachers incline to the methods in which they themselves were trained. This strikes me as natural and probably produces the best results, provided the teacher himself was well grounded; but here is a trap into which many novice instructors fall. It can most easily be recognized in dancers who, after retiring from the stage, open a ballet school and find themselves so imbued with the movements and style they have picked up in their professional years, that any basic knowledge they may have had has long been forgotten. They need a teachers' training course thoroughly revising their knowledge of theory and music and what beginners actually need to know. It is wrong to assume that ultimately every dancer will be able to teach. This misconception contributes to the survival of far too many unqualified instructors who carry on thanks to the ignorance of parents and the apathy of educational authorities.

Dancers who begin teaching without proper pedagogic training are apt to subject children to steps which they themselves can demonstrate with brio but which are beyond the physical capacity of young pupils. These teachers then cannot understand why their insufficiently strengthened pupils do not immediately shine in their reflected light. A certain amount of demonstration is good, especially when an instructor can do this well, but it can become a substitute for real teaching. There is also the danger that a teacher who is more interested in impressing his pupils with his own past glory than in making corrections will lack the real 'eye' to spot talent and promote it. Children, moreover, are especially quick at picking up bad habits and mannerisms. These are two good reasons for not demonstrating too liberally. First, the possibility of a teacher's wasting too much energy on performing instead of reserving strength in order to observe his students more keenly; secondly, the likelihood of pupils copying the imperfections of their teachers. Wonderful exceptions to this are the Grand Old Ladies of the late 'Russian Ballet', a disappearing species, but still to be found in London, Paris and New York, passing on their thoroughbred training by knowledge and example.

Another menace to the teaching profession is the frustrated dancer, who may in fact have no ability to pass on the scanty talent he or she possesses. These dancers have drifted into teaching, not through a desire to instruct after legitimate retirement from the stage, but because they can find no job as a dancer and must somehow keep the wolf from the door.

Perhaps a hidden blessing, where the passing on of knowledge is concerned, is the difficulty of finding a universal method of writing down dancing. Nearly all the well-known teachers of today can trace a direct pedagogical lineage from the great ballet masters of the eighteenth and nineteenth centuries, and until recently classical ballet traditions have been passed from one dancer to another by demonstration and word of mouth. This has in some ways prevented stagnation by allowing for, and incorporating, the great advances in virtuosity and technique expected from every member of a contemporary ballet company. However, in spite of this, I trust that soon one of the several methods of dance notation will evolve, streamlining the considerable complexities (the Benesh System seems well on the way to achieving this), so that the average dancer, and not as at present only specialists, will be able to read and write the mechanics of the art. All technical advances will then be recorded and exchanged throughout the ballet centres of the world.

A great difficulty for ballet schools is obtaining children at an early enough

age for regular classes. The big state schools overcome this by combining normal education with dance training in one establishment, but these academies exist only in the big ballet centres of the world. In Germany, Stuttgart is the first city since the war to own a boarding school for young dancers, but even these children, by German law, have to attend local schools in the vicinity, and dancing classes have to be postponed till the afternoon instead of taking place in the morning before a child's body is fatigued by the day's occupations.

In theory, a pupil should receive two to three classes a week from the age of eight or nine until he or she is twelve, after which four or five classes weekly are definitely necessary. At the age of fifteen or sixteen children with the right physique, talent and character should be selected for further training, but *only* these children, since at this age study becomes so concentrated that further normal schooling is not possible. It is now that the young dancer commences full-time professional study, and in all the good schools this should incorporate a broadening of the basic groundwork to include Modern Dance, Mime, Jazz, Fencing, Character, including the study of Spanish and other National Dances, and exercises in composition. The classical curriculum should incorporate lessons in *pas de deux*, Variations, Repertoire and Theory. Education in History of Dance, Music, Drawing, Dance Notation and Anatomy should also be taken, so that the intellect does not stagnate under the pressure of too many practical classes, and, to take the long view, so that a foundation for later pedagogic study is laid.

So often parents tend to refuse their children ballet lessons until their 'proper' schooling is finished, but of course only very occasionally can a student be successfully plunged into all this activity without the slow preparation of children's ballet classes. This is particularly important for boys, for if the training is condensed into too short a time, the length of a man's professional career is invariably curtailed. If parents would only realize that three classes a week for a boy from ten to sixteen years of age can in no way impair his scholastic studies but can in every way develop his physique, health and athleticism, perhaps they would send their sons to ballet schools more often. The risks are negligible, the gains are great. If at sixteen a boy decides to make dancing his career, he has the enormous advantage of having started to train at the correct age. If, however, he does not then wish to dance, he can concentrate on university entrance exams. Nothing is lost. On the contrary, a properly co-ordinated and harmonious body has probably been developed. How few people realize that the physical education of a dancer is no less athletic than that of a footballer and far more enduring. A good male dancer is at one time sprinter, high jumper, long jumper, weight lifter, ice skater and part-time acrobat, all fused together in the actor-musician.

It is necessary for teachers to have a good understanding of human nature and a sense of humour. The work required in order to gain the essential technique is exhausting and must somehow be squeezed out of children every day. (Whether the pupil or the teacher is more fatigued at the end of a class is a debatable point. Ideally neither should be exhausted; the student should feel physically invigorated and the teacher ready for the next class.) The boundless energy of some children is such that a teacher must sometimes curb too high spirits, but the real test is to get work out of young dancers on the days when enthusiasm is absent. The body needs regular training and cannot rely upon the whim of its owner, so this discipline should

have been started early and have become a habit by the time a dancer enters a professional company. If this is not so, the standard of performance will vary too greatly, the dancer becoming an unreliable member of a ballet, sometimes appearing at rehearsals, sometimes not, according to personal mood. Self-indulgence will quickly nip any career in the bud, especially that of a dancer where physical energy is indispensable to success.

Some children respond to encouragement, others need a challenge or competition. One pupil can best be contacted through the intellect, while another reacts better to music, atmosphere, or other stimuli. All this a teacher must know and understand if he is going to get the most out of his students, but even this is not enough if he does not enjoy their trust and respect. The questioning pupils are often the most intelligent and once these children have been convinced, they normally make the fastest progress.

For any hard, physical work a collective zeal brings the best results; this can usually be engendered by making the bodies of dancers starting class feel warm and supple, and by eliminating any pains from overworked muscles or fatigue. This is especially important when giving company classes where one is usually confronted by a group of adult dancers, all in different states of mind and body, who somehow, without being spoon-fed with individual steps to special people, must in one and a half hours be brought a feeling of agility and the desire to dance prior to satisfactory rehearsal. Of course the really professional company member will understand himself how to benefit from the daily morning class that is his perpetual lot, but very many young dancers, after intensive coaching and preparation before the plunge into a company, will feel themselves lost and neglected for the first year or so unless they have been warned to expect this. I believe that instilling into students the need to care themselves for the well-being of their bodies (and minds) should be an essential part of their education in the last two years of their ballet school training.

A good class consists of two integrated, but in fact quite different, pedagogic demands. One is teaching, the other training, and neither is sufficient without the other. All living things, from fleas and plants to monkeys and children, can be trained by systematic repetition to perform in a desired manner within their limitations, albeit with varying degrees of success depending upon the quality of the raw material (I am sure there are talented and less talented fleas), and a dancer's body is no exception. The limbs and muscles during daily work gradually absorb a shape and discipline which is the fruit of years of training. Teaching, however, imparts a knowledge of the subject, and while it can shorten the period necessary for training a dancer, it cannot in itself produce a disciplined body. Let me give a small example. If the use, purpose, and functioning of say a *grand battement* is explained to a child in great detail and then physically corrected by making the pupil feel the necessary muscles and control points with which to perform the movement, he will probably understand what has to be done, but he will not have mastered a *grand battement*. If, on the other hand, the movement, without explanation, is performed twenty or thirty times, some of the correct muscles will have felt what has to be done, and the student will have added a little strength to his body, though probably no refinement or comprehension.

Surely in most cases the essential aim is to place the brain in the whole body (as opposed to the head alone) and then give the child a functioning machine on which this intelligence can be used.

36

The structure of an advanced class usually consists of four sections: the *barre* work; centre practice and *adage*; *allegro* and *petite batterie*; and finally *grands sauts* and steps of bravura. Though the balance may vary, it is always beneficial to include these four divisions to a greater or lesser degree in each class. In no circumstance should the last section immediately follow the *barre*.

Working tension in classes should not be confused with nervous tension. There is a very real danger of the latter causing physical injuries to dancers by contracting the tendons and dislocating natural co-ordination. How often one sees the over-conscientious pupil building incorrect muscles by tense and nervous straining to do well, while the phlegmatic type with loose joints and relaxed muscles would be so much more successful with a little more 'working' tension. Laughter is a marvellous antidote to that 'up tight' feeling and a good joke in class can do wonders for the atmosphere, providing it is shared by the whole class and is not at the expense of one member or enjoyed by only a giggling few. Teachers should remember that children, living fully in each concentrated day, have a will to succeed beyond adult proportions simply because so much importance is attached to the moment. It is therefore easy to wound the pride and dignity of these young people, but they can be helped by showing how much fun there can be in genuine hard work. Most children are quick to see a joke, providing they are not afraid to laugh, so if the right example is given, the desired atmosphere will create itself.

Teachers should also guard against becoming too involved in the problems of one pupil so that the concentration of other members of the class is lost. Real difficulties, needing private coaching, must be dealt with after class. However, individual attention is a must, and all good teachers know the extra effort pupils will make if they feel they are being personally watched and helped. Perhaps the best teachers and the ones with the most control are those that the pupils can least predict. They should have humour, patience, and logic; they must distribute information, admonition, encouragement and advice; and they must in addition be endowed with knowledge, sincerity, strength and a boundless love of dancing and dancers.

To return to the metaphor I used at the beginning of this chapter, a dancer is a pearl among men, and is worth all the care and cultivation needed to produce this phenomenon.

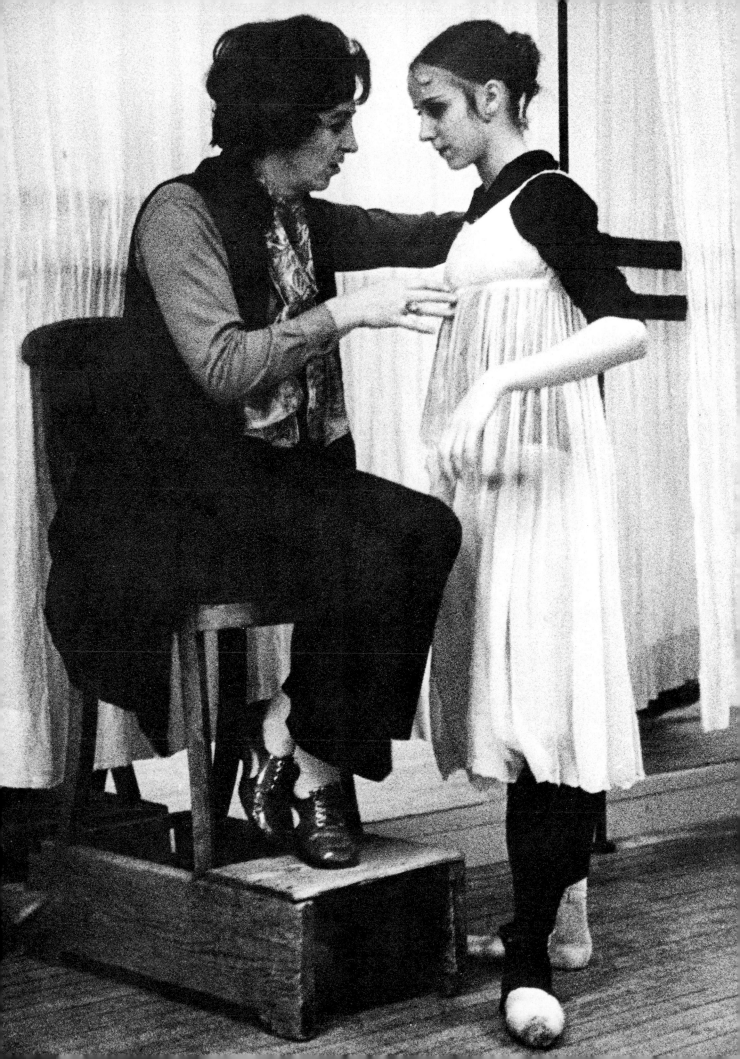

3. Practice Clothes

Costly thy habit as thy purse can buy,
But not expressed in fancy; rich not gaudy
For the apparel oft proclaims the man.

Hamlet

What Polonius lacked in humour he made up for in 'sensible' advice, and though following his recommendations too rigidly would have made Laertes a prig, or an artist of today colourless on the stage, it is nevertheless all sterling stuff and an appropriate warning to the chrysalis dancer who must be preserved from excesses in order to emerge the more gloriously later on.

If one is recognized by one's clothes, then a dancer who looks like one goes part of the way in convincing people of his merit, and indeed, if apparel proclaims the man, a change of apparel proclaims a different man. Just as it is well known that on the stage an actor subconsciously assumes the postures and movements dictated by the limitations of the costume, so is this true of dancers. What better then, than to change into ballet clothes and feel like a dancer?

For example, the basque of a modern *tu-tu* gives the dancer's body a long-waisted feeling that helps to prevent a weak break in the middle, and with the legs fully exposed and enhanced by the short skirt, a special tautening in the knees and feet is automatic. Conversely, in a long hanging skirt it is natural for the lines to become more plastic, the waist is freed, more *plié* is used and a flowing quality, utilizing and complementing the movement of the dress, is the result. So it will be seen, consciously or unconsciously, the costume does have an influence on the way dancers hold themselves and move.

I believe this applies equally to the classroom, and not only from the morale-boosting point of view of looking good and feeling good.

Clean tights without wrinkles at the knee, 'costly as thy purse can buy,' give the legs an important, pulled-up feeling; and a well-fitting and attractive tunic, leotard or shirt makes the dancer look groomed and ready for work. Even the line at the neck can shorten or enhance this part of the body and students will do well to consider this. Polo necks for example are particularly unflattering to anyone with high or square shoulders and also impart a disturbing nuance of amateurism to the wearer. Short skirts with a circular cut can also be disastrous over generous hips; and frills are, without qualification, criminal. Ideally, nothing should break the line of the dancer's body either by juxtaposition of ill-chosen colours or by the added bulges of sleeves or skirts. Even a too tightly pulled-in belt can cause the diaphragm and hips to bulge out above and below the waist and break the length and purity of the torso. It follows that wrist-watches, bracelets, ear-rings and other gew-gaws will only interrupt and irritate and should never be worn during training or rehearsal. I am not suggesting that to look like a dancer is the answer to all problems but simply that the neat prepared feeling 'rich not gaudy, nor expressed in fancy,' is an advantage.

Some dancers will prepare themselves with great trouble and care and yet arrive at a feeling non-advantageous to work. These are the students with real or imaginary small injuries, who wind themselves around with woollen football socks

on the ankles, sweaters tied by the arms round the waist and scarves festooned round 'sore' throats. The result is visually a grotesque mess of knitted appendages, and psychologically a semi-invalid feeling of either self pity or, more often, an attitude of 'you-had-better-be-sorry-for-me-because-I-am-doing-this-class-in-extreme-physical-pain-and-enduring-it-because-of-my-doughty-nature.' Real injuries should be bandaged under medical supervision. (There is a correct and an incorrect way of binding the ankle for example.) The body should, of course, be kept warm while working but never in an ostentatious or ineffective manner. Sometimes it is sheer laziness which results in a dancer's appearing in class as if dressed by an old clothes jumble sale. Possibly the best prevention, if the dancer is not sensitive enough to see for himself what an absurd figure he is cutting, is for teachers to insist upon complete uniformity during the childhood years of training and to strictly enforce rules of neatness. In later years this could be tedious and constricting to the personality so that it is surely better to instil some sort of aesthetic refinement early and then 'free' the dancer to his own choice of colour and shape, hoping his previously fostered good taste will not desert him.

TIGHTS

Personally, I strongly discourage black tights, as the leg becomes a silhouette and loses three-dimensional form by which a teacher can better discern the action of the muscles. Many girls feel black is slimming, but I am not convinced of this. Even if it were so, the dancer does not gain much by creating an illusion for herself in the class-room mirror and on the stage revealing the horrible truth. It would be better to achieve the opposite—unadorned reality battled with daily in the classroom and illusion in performance.

When woollen tights or leg-warmers are worn over nylon stretch tights, the dancer must be wary of a false warmth. It is possible to do *barre* in them, and during pauses in rehearsals they should always be put on, but one can become too 'woolly' on the legs, relying on an external comfort and misjudging it for the necessary warmth engendered by preparatory exercises in the muscles of the leg itself. In general, when the skin surface is cool, blood is pumped more rapidly through the body and feeds the sinews in a natural and healthy manner. Dancers can best judge this themselves. If after the *barre* they take off their leg-warmers before starting the centre practice and find their legs suddenly cold and brittle, they must know their *barre* work has been an illusion—in other words, no work at all.

If thick tights are worn in order to take off weight by perspiring more freely, care should be taken not to overdo this dubious method. Rubber or plastic sweat pants are particularly dangerous, as the skin, unable to breathe, perspires profusely but entirely without engendering warmth in the muscles, thereby not only increasing the risk of injury, but also so debilitating the body that the dancer's energy is severely sapped. To perspire is natural and healthy, and usually oils the dancer's body, making performance easier, but to indulge in this form of slimming brings very slow results, for when the first glass of water is drunk after strenuous exertions, all the liquid previously lost returns to the body. I am also not in favour of track suits. Not only do all sorts of sloppy habits creep in unseen beneath those baggy trousers but also, because they do not fit the leg as tights, they are always constricting. However huge they may be, or however stretchable the material, pressures are brought upon the knee when it is bent, and upon the thigh muscles when the leg is lifted. They should really only be worn for relaxing between rehearsals and never put on over wet practice clothes.

LEOTARDS

Tunics for girls may depend on the dancer's preference. Pale colours are the most attractive and the most professional. Certainly at stage calls, pink tights and pale uncluttered tops must be worn. This is particularly important when rehearsing in front of black curtains, because dancers working in dark clothes will not be properly visible from the auditorium. Men should also avoid wearing black or dark practice clothes for the same reason and should have plenty of clean white vests, shirts and socks at hand for frequent changes during the day.

Most girls wear nothing beneath their tights, as pants can break the line of the leg if they should show below a leotard, and brassieres are worn only if the bosom needs support. Many dancers are comparatively flat-chested as girls more generously endowed usually engage in less active pursuits; or is it that a sufficient number of *entrechat six* will reduce any breast?

Boys need well fitted jockstraps and, from the very beginning, they should buy these in professional dance shops. Some girls also wear elastic jockstraps (sometimes called dance belts), although this habit is dying out. I personally feel they give support to the lower abdomen during strenuous 'lifts', and *pas de deux* in general, and are to be recommended. The feeling of constriction a girl often experiences when first wearing a dance belt is often because she has been working incorrectly with the pelvis, so there can also be technical advantages in wearing these light elastic jockstraps.

Other rules are: no last-minute repairs with a safety pin which can seriously hurt a partner should it open; no belts or buckles which can also scratch; and no elastic belts for girls, which slide up from the waist to the ribs, affording no grip for a man when lifting. Wash practice clothes frequently, make sure of personal hygiene, wear no loose or sharp bits and bobs, and all will be well.

HAIR

The way in which dancers fasten their hair for class and rehearsals varies with the current mode, and this is right. It is important to look attractive and also to have a contemporary feeling for what is happening outside the confined world of the ballet studio. The only rules that do not change are those ensuring that the hair, in whatever style it is worn, stays in place. This means for girls that grips and hairpins should be firmly fixed, ensuring that they cannot fly out, perhaps in the eye of a partner, and that bands or handkerchiefs round the head must be securely tied. Hairnets are seldom used these days as most girls have long hair, making it possible to catch all wisps in a knot at the back of the head. But under no circumstances whatever should hair be allowed to hang loose upon the shoulders. As hair has become longer for men, so has the need arisen for them also to find a means of preventing it flying in the face whilst turning and jumping. A band around the brows usually suffices, looks very 'Olympian', and is worn by many boys today.

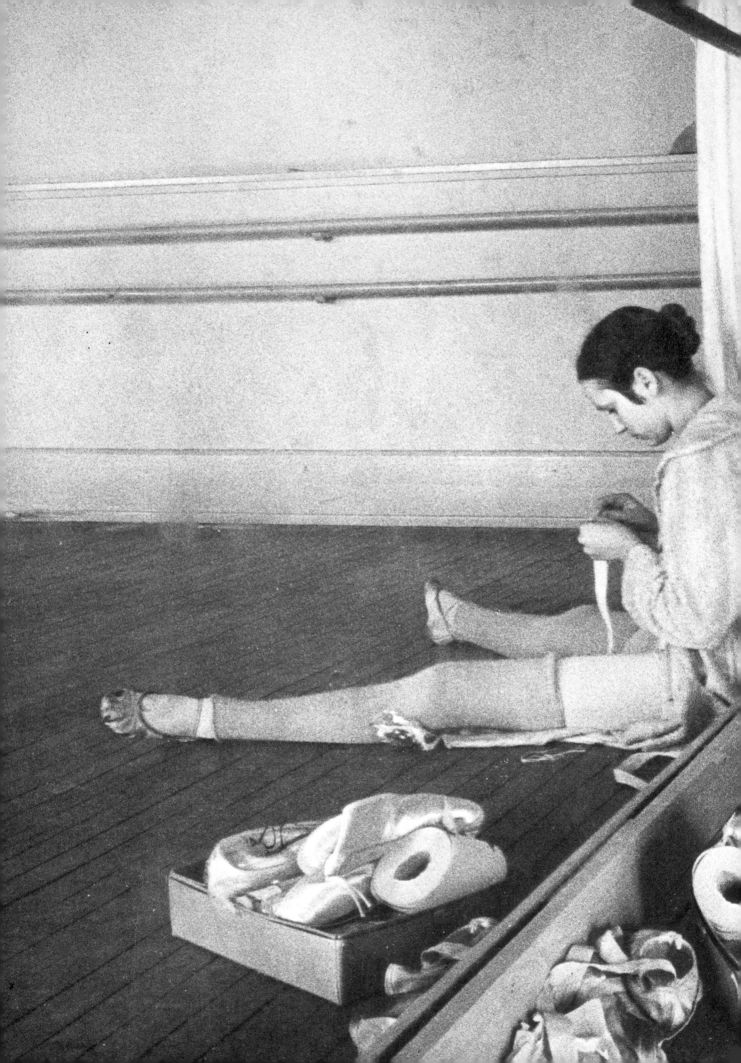

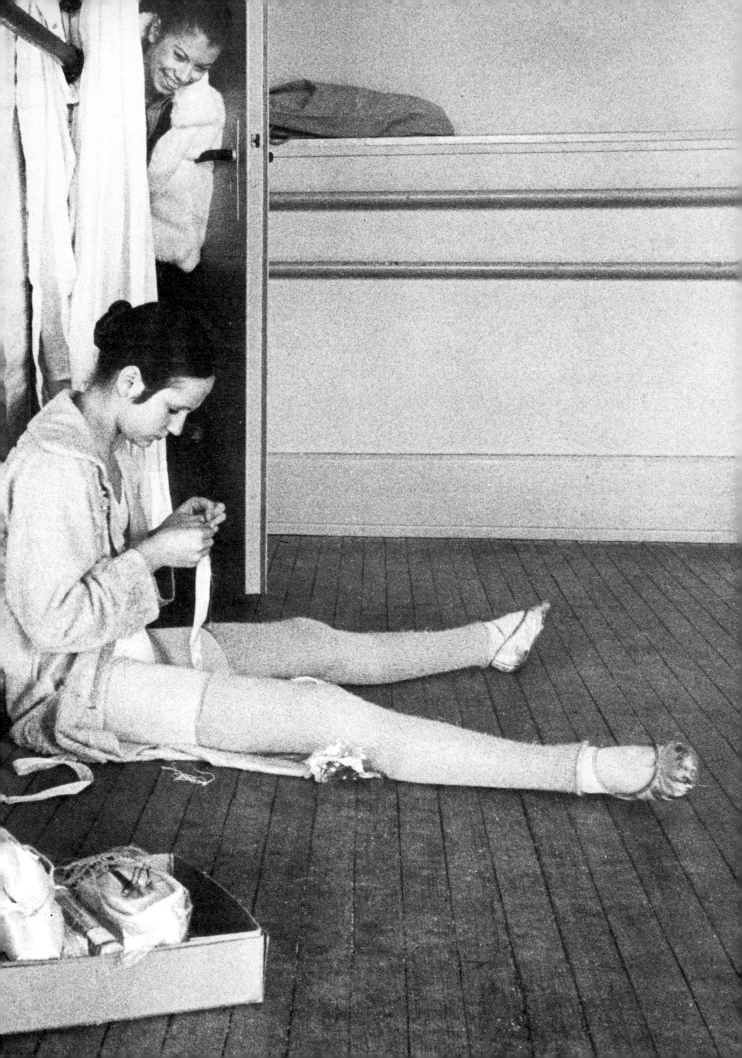

Before entering a ballet company, dancers should have learnt how to dress their own hair in various styles for the stage. In the big opera houses hairdressers are still available, but this is not always the case, and certainly not on tour where a *corps de ballet* girl who cannot prepare her hair, wig or headdress without assistance is not really professional in the dancers' world. Nearly all experienced dancers know the useless feeling of hairpins inserted by someone else. Not only will a loose headdress fall off after the first pirouette, but also the scalp will miss that secure feeling of contact with a well placed hairpin! One does not wear a hat or wig when dancing; it becomes part of the head.

SHOES

Perhaps the most important item worn by any dancer are shoes, as when these are not absolutely correct and comfortable, performance must suffer. Soft shoes should fit like a second skin. For practical training purposes the best are made from good-quality pliable leather, as this is more serviceable than a too-soft buckskin shoe which is often worn by male dancers in performance. Russian soft shoes for boys are made of canvas and are pleasantly light and flexible but they are no longer generally manufactured in Western countries. Size is all-important as too large a shoe is sloppy and dangerous, and one too short will cramp the toes.

POINTE SHOES. Every dancer must experiment until she finds the make and fit that suits her best. (In general, the well-known firms with a good reputation are most to be trusted.) Again, these shoes must fit perfectly, allowing no room inside for cotton wool or rubber toe-caps. They must hold the toes and big toe joint firmly together without bending the knuckles of the toes. Experienced dancers seldom suffer from blisters, and beginners do so only when their shoes are too big and allow their toes to rub up and down (that is, fall forwards into the point of the shoe when standing *sur les pointes* and towards the heel when standing on the flat foot). Nylon tights can also be unhealthy and give rise to sore places, especially on feet that perspire quickly. Every precaution should be taken to avoid blisters: prevention is so much better than cure.

Too hard a shoe is also damaging, as it prevents supple movements in the foot. I am in favour of a firm glove-like feeling, with only sufficient stiffening to prevent the toes from buckling. Precise and sensitive work can hardly be expected from a foot rigidly encased in an unbendable shoe. Quite apart from this, illusion is completely destroyed when a vision of supposed weightlessness can be heard clonking across the stage like a one-man band.

An elastic sewn into the back of the shoe to prevent it from falling off the heel is dangerous, as it can constrict the proper working of the Achilles tendon. If extra security is needed here (and with a properly fitting shoe it should not be) the shoe can be glued or stuck on with spit and resin.

The inside ribbon should be sewn slightly further forward than that on the outside and should also be a little longer in order that the knot may be tied more easily in the correct place. This is not directly at the back of the ankle, where it can bruise the Achilles tendon, but in the hollow between that tendon and the inside ankle bone.

The knot should then be pushed downwards in this groove until it is entirely invisible beneath the other ribbons. These should never become pulled into creased bands but always be laid flat across the ankle. A good method for keeping them ironed is to pull a tautly held ribbon several times across the top of a lighted electric bulb. It is disturbing to see tapes cutting the line of the foot and leg, and therefore shiny satin ribbons are seldom used any more, but rather those made of a strong nylon that will blend with the dancer's tights and remain invisible.

It is also pleasing when shoes are darned on the points. A quick and practical way is to sew concentric circles of blanket stitch, using a fairly tough crochet cotton. Make sure the stitches pick up the undercovering of cotton and then finally cover with glue to give a hardwearing surface. Apart from preserving the satin and preventing it from tearing or rolling up away from the toe, it provides a time for the dancer to get to 'know' her shoes and care for them. This good habit was prevalent in Europe until the 1950s but it has now become very rare for dancers, or even students, to spend so much time on their shoes. Certainly the wearers are no less fastidious, and their anguished cries of complaint over bad shoes do not diminish, but it is a fact that, just as clothes today are bought, hung on the body, and thrown away without sentiment, so point shoes receive no more deferential treatment. It is not unusual for the principal dancer in a three-act ballet to require three pairs of shoes during the evening, and it is true that the shoes manufactured nowadays are not built to last, but many dancers forget that with a little care and 'rest,' shoes recover. When a point shoe becomes slightly damp through the foot's perspiration, it will very quickly soften, but if pulled into the correct shape with newspaper stuffed into the toes and left for a few days, the shoe will again support the foot efficiently. It follows that all dancers should have a reserve stock of shoes, both used and new, so that during rehearsals frequent changes can be made.

There seems to be some significance in the fact that dancers who trained and worked during the years between 1939 and 1946, when point shoes were exceedingly difficult to buy, acquired incredibly strong feet. Surely this means that without the support of new shoes the muscles in the feet became abnormally developed in order to cope unaided with the weight of the body, and that now, in times of plenty, this is a lost advantage. Of course every possible device was used to stiffen old shoes with shellac or 'straw hat dye'. I knew one dancer who had invented a method of washing and baking her shoes which, she insisted, returned them to a state of virginity. But this system failed miserably when I tried it myself, and I cannot recommend it. In fact, satisfactory or not, the stiffening processes we adopted still did not prevent our dancing on point with the big toes sometimes visible through the top of the shoe. An interesting reflection on this period is that, although the girls had strong feet and could run and jump on point better than the average *corps de ballet* girl of today, most of them did not have beautiful feet in the classical sense. Of course there were exceptions, but the long slender foot with a highly developed arch often could not survive the lack of a good supporting shoe. So it is that circumstances, as well as fashion, condition the type of dancer each decade produces.

4. Barre Work

For well over a hundred years, generations of dancers in every part of the world have begun their ballet classes *à la barre*. It is a sobering thought for teachers, when they place a child for the first time with one hand on this wooden rail, that this daily discipline will continue with the dancer throughout his or her entire professional life. Indeed it is an action of some moment and can be said to lay the foundation of a dancer's whole future technical development; but, in spite of the undoubted importance of this work, I am sceptical of dancers professing to love *barre* work. The pianist who can only produce scales is a bore, and the kitchen help who remains satisfied washing the vegetables will never become a chef. Likewise, the real dancer knows that *barre* work helps to gain and maintain technique and is a necessary preparation for performance but that it fills no other function. Nevertheless, if preparation makes an important contribution to the final result—as indeed it must—then *barre* work is to be respected but not necessarily adored.

Some of the good, and most of the bad habits we acquire as children follow us into later life, and therefore the responsibilities of a teacher moulding the physique and perhaps personality of a young person are immense. I think the majority of teachers, who have themselves passed through a long and habit-forming training in the unbroken tradition of classical ballet, are very aware of this and pass on their knowledge with the utmost care and conscientiousness.

It sometimes happens, however, that less experienced instructors, excited by quick results, do not sufficiently consider the long-term effects of their methods; and it is here we encounter the forced and precocious ballet baby, who invariably burns out his or her talent before it can mature. With proper anatomic knowledge this can be avoided. Patience is necessary, but a good teacher need not get bogged down in dry, established customs of the past. While still following traditional principles, he will manage to retain spontaneity and interest during the work at the *barre,* at the same time incorporating exercises devised to help the student deal with all the technical advances currently being made.

It may seem a contradiction in terms to speak simultaneously of unbroken traditions and incorporating what is new, but it is a fact that every living art builds on past foundations and thus avoids stagnation. So it is with the training of young dancers. Making them thoroughly familiar with the tenets and conformities of classical ballet is the best way to help them achieve the fine, highly disciplined instrument that is the dancer's body and also give them a solid base on which they, as the next generation of performers, must build.

Making a position with the body is like making a dress. The material must first be laid flat without creases. Then the shape is cut and the form given with the minimum of tucks and gathers. When the material is pulled and creased before starting, the dress will never be fresh. In fact all exercises should be placed before strength is added. It should not be forgotten that a placed position includes correct carriage of back, arms and head, and not only the lower half of the body. All exercises should be given with great attention to the movements of the upper back, neck and eyes especially as this is where faults and bad habits so quickly manifest themselves.

Daily exercises for serious students and professionals always begin with *pliés* as these have been proved to be the most beneficial and safe way of first exercising the legs. However, many experienced dancers and advanced pupils will arrive in the studio in good time before the class starts in order to 'warm up'. This consists

of gently stretching ligaments where each dancer feels it is necessary and bringing the blood to circulate evenly and thoroughly through the limbs. A teacher should assist students without sufficient knowledge of their own physique by giving them warming-up exercises personally suited to their own bodily problems, which they can perform alone without harm. Also beneficial before a class are deep breathing exercises and moments of stillness to help concentration and relax the body.

After the *pliés,* the *barre* can then be said to work up through the feet, *battements tendus,* etc.; to knees, *battements frappés,* etc.; to hips, *grands battements* and finally to stomach and back muscles, *développés and stretches.* Exercises should alternate in speed and arduousness throughout. Slow for strength and control; fast for brilliance of execution. Great care must be taken, however, especially in later training, that too much energy is not expended during this part of the class, thereby leaving insufficient strength for the more demanding centre practice. How often one sees a clean and correct *barre* followed by totally inept and disappointing work in the centre. This reveals a misunderstanding of the purpose of *barre* work, which is essentially a preparation in all senses of the word. In early training, and in certain cases of physical immaturity, it is to be expected that a young person will be better controlled with the added support of the *barre,* but it should be remembered that it is only a means to an end, even though, as already stated, the greater importance attached to the 'means', the more significant the 'end' is likely to be.

A common fault, and one to be constantly corrected, is that of pulling on the *barre.* No matter how hard or well the student is working, if he cannot at all times release this support and remain balanced over the leg upon which he is standing, his exertions are of no avail. I therefore prefer to work as soon as possible from fifth, as in this position the weight of the body falls over the entire foot, whereas when one leg is raised from the first position, the body cannot remain still and balanced over the other but must shift the weight towards the toes of the supporting foot.

The hand should be lightly placed on the *barre* and slightly in front of the elbow, which should not fall behind the body causing the shoulder to poke forward. This helps to steady the balance and should do away with strains engendered in the neck through grim determination to achieve correctness lower down. The support of a *barre* allows a student to concentrate on one thing at a time and imparts the quiet discipline which places a classical dancer apart from his frenetic fellows. Just as without silence sound does not exist, so without stillness there cannot be movement. Therefore, if dancing is the art of expression through movement, without repose it is itself negated. Dancers must possess tranquility in the body if their actions are ever to convey anything, and what better time can there be to instil this serenity than during the preparatory exercises of the daily class?

The *barre* can also assist the beginner to a greater 'turn-out' than is possible in the centre without support. Reasons for placing the legs *en dehors* in the hip socket are frequently misunderstood and its practice is much abused. It is of no advantage whatsoever to turn the feet alone to an angle of 180 degrees and believe one is turned-out. On the contrary, it can do considerable damage to the knees and spine. A child or dancer, who is allowed to turn his feet outwards to a greater extent than the turn of the thigh in the hip socket allows, has been ill-trained. This is extremely dangerous as it weakens the feet, causes a vicious twist in the knee ligaments, displaces the base of the spine, and often results in a permanently hollowed back. True 'turn-out' takes place just below the pelvis, and all forms of 'sticking' the feet out, such as using water or resin, should be discouraged. A 'turn-out' with the feet at an angle of 180 degrees should be demanded only from advanced students, or from children with legs placed exceptionally *en dehors* in the hip joint. Much better is the request, 'Knees over the little toes please,' which is a phrase that should become familiar to all beginners and ensures that children learn to turn out in the correct place.

If the turning of the leg *en dehors* can be anatomically dangerous and is in any case a troublesome cultivation, why does it occupy a place of such importance in classical ballet? There are several good answers. The first reason is historical: the desire for elegance. The feet were seldom turned further than an angle of 90 degrees from each other, but great importance was attached to their placing, and it was considered both ill-bred and boorish to neglect the cultivation of this refinement. Queen Elizabeth I actually required Ambassadors to the Court of England to dance before she would receive them. The mind boggles at the thought of this custom being continued today, though it would surely be an added distinguishment for the diplomatic corps and one we should heartily welcome. To practised observers the body cannot lie; it would be entertaining, perhaps enlightening, if politicians would conduct their election campaigns by dancing.

The second reason for 'turn-out' is balance. A person standing on one leg has better three-dimensional contact with the floor if the foot is slightly turned out than when the heel is pointing directly backwards. From a technical point of view the advantages are enormous. A dancer standing in the fifth position with the feet correctly placed has distributed the weight of the body in the smallest area possible on the floor. If one leg is raised from this position, the body has the least adjustment to make in order to bring the weight over the other foot, in fact only a matter of the width of the foot forward or back. On the other hand, standing with the feet parallel to one another, the toes facing forward, the hips must make a marked sway to one side if the balance is not to be lost when raising one foot. Whilst performing steps on point the added discipline of controlling the thigh in the hip joint also improves balance and gives pirouettes greater stability.

Another advantage of 'turn-out' is that it enables the legs to be lifted higher by freeing them in the hip joint. Standing again with the feet parallel, it will be found the leg cannot be lifted very far to the side. Should the limb however be rotated outwards, a far wider angle can be reached. This is also true when lifting the leg at the back in arabesque.

As if all these needs for working *en dehors* were not enough, a still further benefit, and perhaps the most important of all, is the resulting purity of line. To give only one example: an arabesque line broken by the knee hanging down or the heel appearing on top cannot be aesthetic and will certainly disturb the visual sensitivities of those believing in the tenets of classical ballet.

'Turn-out' therefore has four established *raisons d'être:* elegance, balance, greater freedom of the legs in the hip socket, and purity of line.

Gentle persuasion is much better than force. A dancer will sometimes find that too much determination to overcome a persistent physical failing is in itself aggravating the fault. For example, a high *développé* is exceedingly strenuous for someone with short ligaments in the groin, and no amount of repetition or strength will place the leg higher than these ligaments allow. On the contrary, the strain imposed creates muscles to deal with the weight of the limb, which then become too large and literally prevent the leg from being held in a high extension. If this happens it is necessary to stop the exercise for a few weeks while the muscles relax, meanwhile regularly stretching the tight tendons till the leg can be lifted more freely. When this is accomplished, the now more supple muscles can be called into use to sustain the position.

Stretches for the whole class should come at the end of the *barre* and only when the body is warm and supple. It is, however, as already mentioned, a good idea for each student to prepare himself before the beginning of the lesson, exercising gently any obstinate physical fault. This is especially necessary with bad 'turn-out' or stiff feet, and the student will derive much more benefit from *pliés* and *battements tendus* if he can pass through the correct positions during these exercises without too much cramping force.

I should like to mention here a particular 'turn-out' stretch I have often encountered, and which should on no account be allowed in any classical ballet school, for it is extremely damaging. This is where a student lies on the floor face downwards and draws up both knees to either side. Unless the student has a complete turn-out of 180 degrees it can only result in the pelvis lifting off the floor, causing a bad curvature in the base of the spine. These exercises must always be performed lying on the back.

A teacher should judge the speed at which steps should be taken according to the fitness of the dancers or the standard of the students. I believe a slow *barre* most benefits children and very experienced and intelligent dancers. In between lies a period where the body must be forced to work hard and fast to gain strength and swiftness, but when this is achieved it is desirable to return to the non-exhausting, correct but simple method of warming up. One notices the truth of this time and again by observing dancers over thirty years of age, who know exactly how to control their bodies and have learnt to conserve energy before performances and yet warm up their muscles efficiently. However, a slow *barre* given to dancers with phlegmatic characters or insufficient knowledge of their own bodies can be a great excuse for 'sleeping' or generally taking it easy, and so teachers must be able to adapt a *barre* to its function and its performer.

Although this work can be varied in multitudinous ways, a traditional order of exercises is nearly always present. Here is a suggested sequence, intended as a basic guide. The actual *enchaînments* can be found in books on theory.

> *pliés*
> *battements tendus*
> *battements glissés*
> *ronds de jambe à terre*
> *battements frappés*
> *petits fondus développés*
> *ronds de jambe en l'air*
> *grands battements*
> *petits battements sur le cou de pied with*
>   *fouettés ronds de jambe en tournant*
> *développés*
> *stretches*

All these exercises should be done with set *port de bras* and head movements increasing in speed and arduousness with the years. Repeats *sur la demi pointe* with double *frappé* and double *rond de jambe en l'air* and, with higher *développé,* can be made according to the capabilities of the student.

In a daily morning class, lasting between one and a quarter and one and a half hours, the normal exercises at the *barre* proceed for about half an hour; but before performances, professional dancers will 'warm up' for roughly twenty minutes, starting their exercises perhaps one hour before the curtain goes up.

In many schools where technically strong dancers are not infrequently produced, an unchanging sequence of steps during the *barre* work is performed daily. Undoubtedly the physical mechanism of a dancer will benefit from the regularity of the exercises, but I am convinced that with an unvaried routine an automatic mindlessness creeps into the execution of the movements; not only will the dancer lose sensitivity, but bad habits will be firmly cemented in. It is arguable that good habits will also be reinforced. This I do not deny; I am just perturbed by the idea of cement in any form in a dancer's body. At the other end of the scale, a complicated and constantly varying *barre* can impose an unnecessary strain on the preparing body by requiring more concentration on the *enchaînement* than upon the correct execution of the steps.

A balanced compromise must be found. Certainly young children should be given a simple but carefully constructed *barre* that can be worked at consistently for perhaps a year with only minor changes. This will give highly-strung pupils a feeling of security and the body will not be hindered by nervous tensions. After five years' regular training in this manner, I think it is beneficial to vary the exercises every week (but not the order in which they occur), so that positions do not become stereotyped and the students are not in danger of making blindly repetitious movements. This mostly concerns the synchronization of head, *port de bras* and *épaulement,* for legs and feet do need, within reason, a repeated series of familiar steps, albeit not forgetting the dangers I have just mentioned. If a teacher can say, 'Today we will place the head in a different position for the *grand battement,*' demonstrate what he wants, and the whole class performs it correctly, he can be congratulated on producing the material for a choreographer's dream company. If a professional dancer has difficulty changing ingrained positions, his work will be seen to be platitudinous and he will be useless to a creative choreographer.

Barre work should be cherished for the great assistance it can give a dancer when correctly used. Not only does it 'place' the dancer without strain in readiness for the more demanding centre practice, but it is indispensable during the early years of training as a preparation for all future advanced work.

5. Head and Arms

The earliest recollection some dancers have of their own arms is lifting them together, with the fingers just meeting above the head, and feeling the elbows brushing their ears. This must have been around the age of three and is a position not likely to last very long with a growing child. However, several decades later, the fifth position *en haut* still looks best when the head is placed centrally in the oval formed by the arms. It lengthens the neck and keeps the shoulders down.

I well remember the soft, small roundness of Lydia Kyasht's arms. She would place them *en couronne* with no trace of an angular elbow or broken wrist and, with the sweetest of smiles, would pass down the *barre* of perspiring students, dropping us words of encouragement. 'Darrlink,' she would coo, with no change in her angelic expression, 'you look like Fat Cow.' She taught us to smile while working, even if we felt like weeping; and though perhaps it is no longer desirable to catch the eye of a Czar, it is certainly to be preferred to the very grim expressions seen on the countenances of some dancers today.

The shape the arms are making can, and should, change the tilt of the head, the light and shade on the face and the expression in the eyes. When this happens unconsciously, it lands the dancer on the credit side of the enormous gulf between the technically strong and the technically beautiful. It is a quality without which no dancer can become great. Ideally it should be instinctive, but it can be taught; and it is no less than criminal negligence when, possibly due to today's enormous technical demands, teachers preoccupy themselves with strengthening legs and giving students athletic prowess while ignoring all that happens above the waist.

I love the movements of hand and arm, and I see them as the breath of dancers made visible. They can also, being tell-tale in their exposure of personality, quickly reveal characteristics of individuals.

It is always interesting to hear the observations of people with no technical knowledge of ballet. Often they have a critical faculty undisturbed by admiration for minor stunts, and from their objective viewpoint they can give dancers direct and astringent advice. In normal conversation it is more natural to look at the face of the person you are speaking to than the shape of their insteps. Criticism from outsiders is often as straightforward as that. They will notice the expression (in the eyes particularly); the grace of the head, hands and arms; and the co-ordinated rhythm of the body. After a time they will become more sophisticated and start talking about 'placing' and arabesques, and the purging effect of their criticism, so beneficial to performers, is lost.

Children, especially, often have a charming and unconscious carriage of the head, governing its movements by the eyes or the thoughts and motives within. Such natural reactions should be encouraged and cultivated and not destroyed by insistence on inclinations that are not spontaneous. It follows that stiff or self-conscious children can be helped more by the suggestion of ideas to which the head responds instinctively than by anatomical explanations of the movement itself. In *effacé*, for instance, the head can be described as turning on one side and sleeping on a cushion just behind the shoulders. In a *brisé dessus* a girl can be told to imagine that she has on a *tu-tu* and must look over the skirt and down if she wishes to see her feet appear for the 'beat'. Very young children can be taught the habit of following the hands with the eyes, and when they do this the proper inclinations of the head will occur automatically. As the ways in which dancers place their heads show personal characteristics, freedom should be allowed for these to develop, providing they remain harmonious. The teacher should, however, be on the look-out for any signs of strain in the face, neck or chin, and these should be checked as soon as they are detected and before they become a habit.

In most cases, movements of the head should be felt as though taking place above the neck. Imagine the spine as a long stem running up from the base of the back with the skull sitting loosely on top. Now place the tip of the index finger on the end of the nose and waggle the head from side to side without letting the finger move and without any tensing of the muscles in the neck. When this movement is quite free, take the finger away and let the eyes and face turn to look directly at any objects other than those straight in front, still letting the neck play as small a part as possible and moving the head as if it wished always to face the sun.

The next exercise is to move the head and neck as though they were hinged only between the shoulders. When the possibilities of both these movements are properly understood, they can be used in choreography to profoundly significant effect. To give one example from a classical ballet, the supple neck motions made by the Swan Queen after the first arabesque following her entrance in the second act of 'Swan Lake' can, if the dancer has an expressive head, establish the whole character of Odette.

The muscles holding the head erect are some of the strongest in the body and are at work at all waking moments. It is therefore not surprising that unless a dancer is made aware from the beginning of the need to develop other muscles to deal with strenuous movements, the neck will automatically play a large part, and the dancer will show unpleasant strain, probably developing unsightly sinews either side of the throat.

In the chapter on mime, I have written about facial expression and its ability to charm and to reveal emotion. This is very important but it is not the only function of the head: it also plays an important role in co-ordinating the technique of the body. Obviously the first use that springs to mind is 'spotting' in pirouettes, where it is essential that the head should turn sharply in advance of the body. To prove how this stabilizes the equilibrium and prevents giddiness, one has only to turn round several times with the head held still to feel the result of not focusing on a constant spot after each revolution. There are also other balances that depend upon the eyes. When performing on a raked stage, a dancer will focus slightly higher than usual, thus throwing the weight back. Conversely, if a dancer looks slightly lower than forward while sustaining balances (during *pas de deux* the *attitude promenades* in the 'Rose Adagio' are a good example), the weight remains forward over the supporting leg. In most allegro work and in all fast changes of direction, the eyes and the 'mind' should clearly fix on parts of the room to give the movements a feeling of purpose and to give shape and direction to the steps. An oculist will often recommend exercises to keep the muscles of the eye healthy, and it is a good idea for dancers to follow this advice by moving their eyes as far as possible from side to side and up and down and by rolling them in the sockets. Children enjoy doing this, and it need not take up more than a few minutes every day in their classes.

The manifold possibilities of head, hand and eye movements were first borne in upon me while dancing in India. We were all anxious to see and learn as much as possible about the ancient traditions of Indian dance, and the company took classes from both Uday Shankar and Ram Gopal. We soon became acutely conscious of how unsubtle and almost immobile our hands were in comparison with those of the Indian dancers, and how our eyes and eyelids no longer play a major or, to be more precise, stylized role in our means of expression. The great beauty produced by flexible bodies and attention to religious detail can teach us much, for the classical dances of India have profound refinements largely overlooked by Western dancers. Of course, we must not forget that the technique of classical ballet has evolved out of our own culture, and that although we can enrich our vocabulary by borrowing and adapting from other sources, we should try to avoid producing an incoherent mixture of styles. Indeed, it is dangerous for dancers to dabble superficially in Eastern cultures or religions. These are great mysteries and need total discipline and contemplation. Personally I find it presumptuous and ignorant on the part of dancers to practise insufficiently understood Yoga exercises—to give one example—in the mistaken belief that it will assist their classical technique. Genuine religious belief is a source of strength to any individual and, as a philosophical guide to one's code of behaviour, no less helpful to dancers than to other people; but to use it as a short cut to body control is to misuse it and to pervert its essential truth into something of no more than superficial value.

Some dancers have sensitive and beautiful hands. Too many of them still have ten boring bananas as extensions of their arms. Why should this be, when, as we all must know, fussy or mannered hands are tedious or disturbing and can seriously undermine a dancer's success? Most choreographers can be directly inspired by the special personal gifts of dancers, and hands are no exception. For those so endowed and possessing the ability to interpret ideas, themes and motivations requiring strange movements and creating dramatic effects are conjured up.

If a cultivated and sensitive use of arms, as richly expressive as possible, is what we are aiming for, the first step is to ensure that no bad habits creep into a student's work. A common fault is to let the index finger point and the thumb stick out at right angles to the rest of the hand. This is nearly always an indication of strain denoting a lack of strength in some other part of the body and, apart from everything else, ruins the line of the arm by giving it a visible stop. I shall explain the correct position of the hands elsewhere. To keep them so will ensure a non-aggressive line, but a really harmonious whole needs life and sensitivity of its own and complete co-ordination with the body. Wonderful examples of this are the hands so tenderly portrayed by painters during the Italian Renaissance and I can think of no better study for the student than to absorb their lines until they know instinctively when their own hands become discordant.

Style of arms and their movement varies greatly from country to country, school to school, and of course ballet to ballet. Surely the only 'style' that is right is that which belongs naturally to the ballet being performed: its period, its character and its choreographic demands. Therefore, arm movements learned during training should have an abstract purity upon which style can be built as required. Arm and hand movements caressing the head have almost totally disappeared from the every-day class. This is a pity, as it leaves the hands too remote from the body, separated perhaps by a wooden elbow. The faculty of touch in our fingers is one of the most

sensitive we possess, and the hand can always express tenderness when the fingertips are used to convey the idea of contact, even if only with the air. These soft personal movements are to be found in young children, still filled with curiosity and learning to understand the textures of their environment, but they are sometimes lost when serious training starts and the body fills with tensions and exertions. This is the time for giving them good habits. If the correct classical carriage of the arms and the correct positions when they are in repose become habit, they can later be discarded in the interests of interpretation, but the control and purity will not be lost with the emergence of the artist.

During academic training, neither a stretched nor a bent arm is desirable, and to control the intermediate position with fluidity is, for a beginner, difficult to sense, and for a teacher tricky to explain. The best method is to ensure that the arm is correctly placed *à la seconde* at the *barre*. The arms held thus daily for half an hour will slowly develop muscles to support them, and if they are held still will accustom the lower half of the body to working without the involuntary help of muscular shoulders. The arms should appear boneless and very gently rounded.

All sharp angles, such as elbows or accentuated wrists, should disappear. Stillness should never become rigidity. It can best be compared to a dancer standing in the fifth position. He is in repose and yet the body has tension and is ready for action. So should the arms be vitally alive when still and not subject to compulsive action when other limbs are working.

A usual and beneficial habit to be acquired while moving is that of passing the arms forward through the first position or 'gateway' (sometimes called fifth *en avant*) when taking a position. This prevents them from wildly flying out and upwards on jumps and ensures that the muscles in the back are participating correctly. Provided the hands are the right distance from the body, the effect will be to widen and lower the shoulder blades, simultaneously flattening the back. Insistence, while training, upon the 'gateway' (and incidentally the fifth position of the feet) is the best method for laying a solid clean foundation which, by inoculating the pupil against bad habits, will later stand him in good stead during long rehearsals and routine performances. If the arms are properly controlled from the spine, they will, to a large degree, contribute to the mastery of technically difficult steps. They can also create illusions of effortlessness, lengthen lines, and give swing and impetus to travelling and turning steps.

Because of the complexities of the shoulder joints and their rather obvious faults when they are badly used, many teachers spend much time correcting them and forget, or do not see, that the origin of the trouble perhaps lies elsewhere. It is not at all unusual for a highly strung child to lift his shoulders when nervous, and it is in fact a physical reaction or characteristic easily observed in any person suddenly frightened or lacking self-confidence. There are many psychological causes for 'nervous shoulders', but if children are allowed to work with, this tension and never learn to relax these muscles, it is exceedingly difficult to correct later on.

Sometimes boys will develop high and lumpy or even rounded shoulders by too much heavy lifting in *pas de deux* work and this can best be combatted (if the *pas de deux* really must continue) by trying to distribute the lifting forces more evenly in thighs and back.

At other times the cause of unaesthetic shoulders can be corrected in the elbows.

If the arm is held to the side, with the palm facing diagonally forwards and downwards, it will be found that the funnybone can be turned towards the floor so that when the arm bends, the hand will rise in a curve upwards; or pulled up, so that when the arm bends again it will make a curve downwards. However, as the elbow is not a ball and socket joint it can, anatomically, only bend in one direction with very small articulation sideways. What has really happened is that the upper arm has revolved in the shoulder joint. Therefore, if the elbow is held in a faulty position, it follows that the arm is also incorrectly placed at the shoulder. The most usual mistake is to see the elbow hanging below the wrist when the arm is to the side. This, of course, not only shortens and breaks the line but also creates a further angle at the shoulder joint and does not sufficiently utilize the muscles around the ribs to correct the position. The elbow must be lifted until the arm curves gently down to the hand with no break where the joint could destroy the continuity of the line. If now the arm is bent, the hand should make a horizontal curve forwards.

Some arm movements should actually originate in the elbow. The flying gestures of the arms made by the swans in 'Swan Lake' are perhaps the best-known example. These waves look exaggerated and inelegant when the initial impulse comes from the shoulders, therefore girls should imagine the movement beginning in the elbow, and the wrist and fingers following afterwards.

Before a turn, the elbows can govern the preparation to a large extent; and teachers should carefully observe pirouettes that are falling off balance to see whether it is not in fact the elbow, and consequently the coordination of the shoulders, that is at fault.

From a purely aesthetic point of view, girls should give their elbows attention and beauty care to make sure that they remain white and to postpone the inevitable wrinkled skin which appears above the joint when it is straightened and which may well sabotage the youthful illusion a ballerina is creating.

Apart from the practice of the many beautiful, traditional *ports des bras*, teachers and students should not forget to make a daily habit of exercising the head and neck, eyes, elbows, wrists and fingers individually so that all joints remain supple. Elementary combinations of movements as given to children will suffice, so long as they ensure that the dancer controls separate articulation in all the joints. It is also advisable to give *enchaînements* where the arms do not always synchronize with the rhythm of the feet. A good exercise for this is given in the chapter on *Batterie*. Another combination, more for separate co-ordination than rhythm, is suitable for children after three years training and is performed as follows:

Standing at the *barre,* right foot front. 2/4 or 6/8, 1 *battement glissé* in each position *en croix.* (1, 2, 3, 4).
With the first *battement* the right arm is taken to fifth *en avant.* (1)
With the second to fifth *en haut.* (2)
With the third to *seconde.* (3)
With the fourth the arm returns to fifth *en bas.* (4)
Repeat the four *battements glissés,* but reverse the arms, e.g. (1) *à la seconde,* (2) *en haut,* (3) *en avant,* (4) *en bas.*

Some performers are lucky enough to possess expressive qualities in the upper

part of their bodies and will automatically respond correctly to musical demands or the dramatic needs of the character they are playing. Others need to cultivate this, and, to sum up, I suggest the following to students: begin by cultivating an awareness of the exact position of the hands and anticipate the shape of their path through the air. Follow this up by endeavouring to imbue the arms with actions suitable to the various *enchaînements* in class. (The correct carriage of the arm at the *barre* helps only to perfect the limb itself. The beautiful use of arms is the next step forward.) More than anything else the arms and carriage of the head give style and period to dancing. Therefore do not forget that a small nineteenth century pointwork *enchaînement* does not need long lyrical arms or that, conversely, a classic *adage* can be ruined by insufficiently stretched arms or affected hands and wrists.

The arms, hands, head and eyes can all assist a dancer by technically aiding balance and by aesthetically perfecting line, but, even more important, they are the most eloquent aid to communication, which is, after all, what ballet is about; therefore, when used with instructive intelligence, they help to express more clearly the ideas of choreographers.

6. Adage

The term *adage* comes from the Italian *adagio,* and though it is generally accepted as meaning 'slow', the musical dictionary gives the definition of the word as 'at ease'. This is a marvellous paradox when applied to ballet, as nothing is more difficult or requires greater strength and control than slow movements well performed. This other meaning of *adagio* should not be forgotten, however, as it is just this quality of effortlessness that a dancer should seek to convey.

All signs of strain or endeavour destroy the graceful and leisurely atmosphere in which the spectator should participate.

It is now that the dancer displays the perfection of his line, and for this reason alone, nothing must upset the harmony of a position. An over-extended finger, just as much as faulty placing in the hips, can detract from an otherwise pure arabesque, probably because in *adage* little can be helped, or hidden, by cheating. In fact, so much is required to be correctly placed that teachers should guard against giving too many instructions all at once. A student can only concentrate fully upon one thing at a time, and this means that the physical perfecting of *adage* is a slow methodical process of gaining strength and good habits.

The best 'line', however, is really achieved by thought! By this I mean concentration on the abstract character of the position. The technical details of placing should be dealt with at the *barre,* and after a few years the student should not need minor corrections pertaining to unstretched feet, lumpy hands, or twisted pelvis and shoulders. Once all the laws governing the posture of the body are observed by force of habit, the dancer will find that if he understands the 'spirit' of the position he will be able to master it physically and technically. If a dancer is filled with the idea behind a movement, all parts of his body will react concordantly. That is half the battle, the rest is achieved by strength and reserves of technique.

In classical ballet *adage* is often associated with the slow movement of the *pas de deux,* in which it firmly states the sovereignty of the dancers, but this is by no means the only manner in which it can be used. Unhurried movements should be able to express solemnity, wonder, melancholy, ecstasy, peace and tenderness, not to mention apathy and fatigue. There are many possible interpretations of slow movement, but the control which is required of classical dancers when displaying the lineal purity of which only they are capable, is what, in its abstraction, most nearly reaches the sublime.

In a wide and noble attitude the eyes look out clearly and directly. The body feels free and extended, and the position radiates outwards. As soon as the eyes drop, the head will also incline and the line becomes softer and more introverted. Similarly, a dancer focusing firmly on a spot on the wall, in order to maintain the balance, will cut short the line of the position, however long the limbs may be, by giving a boundary to the thought. If an arabesque is not to stop at the fingers and toes, it can only be given a feeling of infinity if the eyes have this idea behind them. Vision plays an important part in balancing. I therefore try to instil into my students the belief that they can develop a second pair of eyes in the lower part of the back, which then, by 'seeing', can control and secure the equilibrium, leaving the real eyes free to convey emotion. This form of concentration can be hindered by a too liberal use of the mirror, which, although a traditional part of the furnishing of a ballet studio, can be particularly harmful to beginners. It is quite wrong to focus the attention upon a reflection, thereby relying upon a visual corroboration, in preference to the concentration which

is directed to the centre, or 'control box' of the position. Only by practising the latter can an atmosphere of truth be created, which in turn will impregnate the whole body.

Of all positions in classical ballet the one most easily recognized, and certainly the one most often caricatured, is the arabesque. The uninitiated would-be funnyman, when introduced to a dancer, invariably lunges forward with his body and right arm, lifts the leg rather pathetically *derrière* and, closing his eyes, assumes an expression of seraphic inanity. Relaxing his position and changing the grimace to a leer he asks, 'How would I do?' The dancer bravely joins in the fun and quips, 'You're engaged,' but inside he is bleeding. He has spent fifteen years perfecting his arabesque and this loon, this pagan oaf, defiles what is sacred. I think all dancers react like this, not because they are stuffy, pious or self-righteous, but because their job demands 100 per cent of their energy and devotion and therefore deserves corresponding respect. However, if dancers are sensitive to ridicule they should ensure that their own performance does not invite it.

This beautiful and harmonious position, known in classical ballet as Arabesque, is rich in diversity. Although the height and position of the raised leg gives the more striking impression, it is in fact the back which plays the greater role. The entire symmetry of the pose, from fingertip to toe, is governed by this part of the body; and the more beautiful the back is, the more effect it will have when turned upon the feeble jokes of philistine friends.

The great teacher Vera Volkova used to tell us in class, 'I do not wish to see Mary Smith standing in arabesque, I wish to see "Arabesque" and then look in my programme to find out who had bewitched me.' Certainly there lies a secret here.

It is interesting to ask students to make drawings of various positions in dancing. Even if the dancer has no talent as a draughtsman, it forces the mind to attempt to express itself on paper visually and without words, and this inner knowledge of the desired line can increase a pupil's awareness of form and shape.

Dancers should remember that good *adagio* work is not a question of lifting the legs as high as possible, but that the beauty of a position, however high the extension, is always dependent upon a harmonious whole. The ability to raise the legs freely is of course necessary to dancers, and high extensions can be exciting and beautiful when used for a specific purpose and when the body and arms participate intelligently. But what does a loosely lifted leg achieve when it has no relation to the form? It is merely acrobatic and valueless. If a dancer performing a *développé* has a mental picture of where the leg will be when fully stretched and fully raised and concentrates from the beginning with this in mind, the unfolding of the leg will fill the spectator with expectancy, and the final extension will become a breathtaking realization.

The importance of 'line' in dancing is not confined to the position of the body at a given moment but should also be present in the shape of the movement. In a *grand rond de jambe* the arc that the leg describes in the air should be just as beautiful as the leg itself. Circles are often drawn in dancing and the patterns traced on the ground should bear relationship to those made by the limbs in the air. As early as the beginning of the fifteenth century, Domenico of Piacenza, who wrote the first treatise known to us on the Art of Dance, said: '. . . do not just walk around . . . but give the feeling of the creation of a circle.' In this way, dancing is given a three-dimensional, sculptural quality, combining greater aesthetic perfection than many other art forms. Dancers must also avoid the habit of moving from one static pose to another, often oblivious of ill-timed and ugly connecting movements, which have no relationship to the musical line. Pausing at the height of a position is not incorrect and plants a momentary picture in the mind's eye, but a series of such interruptions becomes monotonous and weakens the dramatic impact.

I believe that the amount of musical sense a dancer possesses can best be discerned in these broad protracted movements. There is greater scope for nuances of rhythm than in the staccato beats of allegro, and a good performer will be able to interpret and phrase the music, bringing it an individual quality of his own. Jumping obviously gives the body a different rhythm from that of prolonged *adage* movements. The heart beats faster, the muscles contract and release at greater speed and there is more excitement and activity. Until a student is capable of recognizing and organizing these rhythms within himself, it is difficult for him to 'calm down' sufficiently for slow balanced work after steps of allegro. It is therefore best to practice *adage enchaînements* shortly after leaving the *barre* when the body is warm and supple and before the *exercises sautés*.

The sustained slow turns executed in *adage enchaînements* require enormous strength and control, and when well-performed have great beauty. They should not be confused with multiple pirouettes requiring perpendicular balance and a sharp head movement, but should rather revolve in a given position or even change the balance of weight and leg and arm positions during the turn. These very exciting and lyric movements were highly developed by the Jooss School and now serve to enrich the classical dancers' vocabulary. Allowing the hips to sway off the perpendicular line from the supporting foot is disconcerting to elementary students, but later on a good dancer should instinctively be able to co-ordinate the weight of the shoulders to harmonize a spiralling turn, with the working leg and arms performing opposing spirals.

From the very beginning, all *développé* should be taught with special attention to the carriage of the torso, the spine always lengthened and undisturbed. Strength in the *upper* back must run in a horizontal line through the centre of the body from a point just below and behind the armpit to a corresponding point on the other side. Strength in the *lower* back should be taken in a perpendicular line, with the sacra pushed well down and not forwards. The back should be thought of as an expanding triangle.

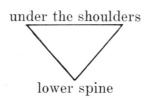

At no time should this create a rigid, immovable feeling. On the contrary, with the strain of work so distributed the spine should be freer to move with grace and control. The waist should be supple and made slender by elongating and not by pulling it in, in the manner of holding a large breath. It must also control a tendency, caused through looseness, of allowing the hips to twist while the upper body remains square.

The stomach should be flat and springy. A stretched feeling over the abdomen can be acquired by making a habit of lengthening the lower back and turning the legs out in the hip sockets without the use of the buttock muscles.

A very good exercise for giving strength to the stomach and back is executed at the *barre*:

Stand with the right foot *pointe tendue en arrière,* the right arm *en haut.* Perform three *grands battlements en cloche,* the third held for count (4) as high as possible, and with the body thrown back in a straight line from the pelvis. Do not let the waist weaken or the supporting leg bend. Repeat: with the count of (4) held in *arabesque penchée,* the arm remaining *en haut.*

To acquire a command of *adage* there is really no better prescription than a dose of *temps liés,* with all its progressing complexities, to be taken daily. Here is a straightforward version of this exercise which is good for the smooth transition from one foot to the other and the controlled descent from half point.

> Music slow 3/4. Fifth position *croisée.* Right foot front. *Fondu* on left leg, right foot *sur le cou de pied devant,* arms fifth *en bas,* head inclined towards back foot. (*1,2,3*)
>
> *Développé en quatrième croisée devant en fondu* arms fifth *en avant.* (*2,2,3*)
>
> Step on to the right foot *sur le demi pointe* and raise the left leg in *arabesque croisée.* The right arm is to the side, the left arm *en haut.* The head is turned to the front and slightly inclined. (*3, . .*)
>
> Remain balanced. (*. 2,3,*)
>
> Descend softly through the supporting foot into *fondu*; the body arms and leg remain in position. (*4,2,3*)
>
> *Coupé dessus.* The left arm comes down to *cinquième en avant,* and the whole body faces front. (*5,2,3,*)
>
> *Développé à la seconde* with the right leg. The left leg *en fondu.* Left arm opens to the second position. (*6,2,3,*)
>
> Step on to the right leg and lift the left leg immediately *à la seconde,* the arms remain in the second position. (*7, . .*)
>
> Remain balanced. (*. 2.3.*)
>
> Close *en cinquième devant.* (*8, 2,3,*)
>
> Repeat on other side.
>
> Repeat both sides *en arrière,* making the first *coupé dessus* the *développé, en arrière croisée,* and the *piqué* in *quatrième croisée devant* with the opposite arm to working leg high.

The soft sustained descent from *demi pointe* to *fondu* is a beautiful melting movement which needs long practice, during which time the muscles surrounding the instep are carefully developed in order to gain the necessary strength. It is especially wonderful when point work has this quality.

'Technical' is a word seldom found amongst the adjectives employed to describe a beautiful dancer; and 'technically a strong dancer' has slight overtones of disparagement. Does this mean 'technique' is a dirty word when ballet is being discussed, that our preoccupation with freedom has caused us so to despise discipline in the performing arts, that only the natural spirits can be accorded homage and respect? This is of course bunkum where ballet is concerned and can only be explained or mitigated by the artist's legitimate howl of anguish at having to live in a technical world. A world, in fact, which grows more technical every day and where the individual feels himself becoming a faceless number within some cosmic computer.

As this book is about ballet and technique, I can only offer as my apology the explanation that I, personally, still find a beauty in 'technical' or academic purity.

7. Pirouettes

The pirouette—a much abused servant of the choreographer! Time and again one has the impression that a choreographer is either at a loss for a step to fill in some music or believes the audience will lose interest unless he supplies a peppering of stunts to keep it awake. And so we have the ubiquitous pirouette. No male dancer today can hope for a place in the corps de ballet of even a moderate sized company unless he can be relied upon to perform three turns with a clean finish, and most soloists turn at least six or more. This essential skill for male dancers has led to a very exaggerated emphasis on the ability to spin, and though used in the proper context, pirouettes are exhilarating to watch, I would suggest that multiple pirouettes alone do *not* make a dancer. (I am, though, the first to applaud a clean and exciting bravura finish to a variation!) By this I do not mean there is no place for the pirouette in good choreography. On the contrary, it is a definite part of the vocabulary of a dancer and can either have an emotional relevance or add abstract shapes and spirals to a ballet according to the deftness with which it is used by the choreographer.

An interesting fact can be observed watching completely untrained children improvising to music, for well over 75 per cent will incorporate turning steps. Young people often spin round and round just for fun, continuously turning in one direction until giddiness throws them on the floor. This early fascination with revolving is found in the folklore of many countries where dances are still performed in circles or utilize rotating steps in pairs or singly, the latter most spectacularly in the frenzied dances of the Dervishes where it has become a means of hypnosis.

Possibly the most famous series of turns in classical ballet is the thirty-two *fouettés rond de jambes en tournant* in 'Swan Lake,' Act III. Multiple *fouettés* were perfected at the end of the last century in the ballet school at Milan and were brought to Paris by Zambelli and to London by Bessone and Legnani. The ballerina Legnani had been executing this stunt, formidable by contemporary standards, for several years before she astounded Russia by performing them as Odile in the first Leningrad performance of 'Swan Lake' in 1895. This was the second production of Tchaikovsky's ballet, destined to become perhaps the most world famous dance drama of all time. Petipa was already an old man and his powers were waning. Tchaikovsky had died in 1893, and this historic production incorporated the second act, as choreographed by Ivanov the year before, in its entirety. In all probability Legnani had no difficulty in persuading Petipa to let her display her legendary turning prowess in the third act, and so the thirty-two *fouettés* were bequeathed to posterity. At all events it was challenge enough to get the whole of the Marinsky School spinning out of sheer provocation, and this particular stunt was soon mastered by many danseuses. It was to remain in the Black Swan's *pas de deux* to this very day, a thorn in the flesh of some of the best Odettes/Odiles, but justified as a stunt by being an indication of the trickery lying within the character of Odile.

Now, when most graduating students manage single and double *fouettés* without too much trouble, one wishes more than ever that it had been possible to make films affording glimpses of legendary dancers. How did Mlle. Heinel, the 'inventor' of the pirouette, use her head? Did Legnani, while performing the thirty-two *fouettés,* make the accent on the *fondu* or on the *relevé?* How big were Grisi's thighs? How did Vestris accomplish the *entrechat dix?* The questions are prosaic, but alas, the magic of past dancers (or present-day ones for that matter) cannot be captured on

film, and the best one can wish for is a record of visual facts, none the less interesting when every morsel of information fascinates.

One thing is certainly true: the male dancer, thanks to his stronger physique, is better able to control a turn than his female counterpart and therefore can afford to give a more forceful push off at the start. Where exactly is his strength so much greater? Mainly in the shoulders, back and thighs and it is the back that governs a pirouette. The ballerina, however, turning on point, has a smaller area of resistance to the floor and can often turn straighter and faster than a man, though she usually loses her (less controlled) equilibrium sooner. This is easily observed by watching girls making multiple pirouettes with the support, often quite nominal, of a partner, while the same dancer only manages two or three revolutions if unsupported. Nearly all dancers turn better to one side than to the other. An interesting phenomenon, and one I should love to have explained, is that the majority of dancers in the West turn better to the right, while those from Eastern Europe seem to prefer spinning to the left. This, I am sure, has nothing to do with politics! It is, nonetheless, fact!

Pirouettes also appear to have a direct connexion with personality, and the impetuous and easily excited dancer will often turn much better, sometimes at the cost of academic clarity, than the cautious over-anxious type. I have also found that short-sighted students sometimes have less trouble when turning, and, since balance depends largely on the eyes (and the ears), I am at a loss to explain this. (It is also a fact, I believe, that deaf people do not suffer from sea-sickness. Can there be a connexion here?)

However, successful turning relies very largely on a knack of timing. Several technical aids are required and rules must be observed, but these all fail when the balance is upset because of faulty rhythmic co-ordination. Let us first examine the technicalities. (The following is given with a *relevé pirouette en dehors* in mind, but the main points apply to all turns.)

1. When a turn is taken from fourth, the weight must be over the front foot during the preparatory *plié*.

2. The heel of the supporting foot must remain on the ground during the preparation in order to make a strong *relevé*. So often in *pirouettes en dehors* from fourth, the front foot is seen to turn in just before the spin begins, causing a misplacement of the hips during the turn.

3. When turning on point, the dancer must give a slight spring to arrive correctly on the supporting foot. This means that on the *relevé* the tip of the toe travels to the point where the centre of the foot had been on the floor, thereby not requiring a transfer of weight. Girls should also practice pirouettes on half point like this, turning with the supporting heel lifted as high as possible (Cecchetti . . . *à trois quarts*), but boys turn on a much lower *demi pointe* and do not require this small spring, as the weight on the ball of the foot is slightly differently distributed.

4. The turning position must be arrived at as soon as possible: for example, when turning *en dehors* from fourth position, the back leg must snap into position immediately and not wait till the body has made half a turn and then lazily join the supporting leg . . . usually rather over crossing the shin bone.

5. The pointed working foot should be placed in front of the supporting leg just below the knee—a little lower for men and also for girls in the case of supported *pas de deux* turns.

80

6. The spine should be held as straight as possible and the pelvis must not tilt. A bad fault, usually caused by weak turn-out in the groin, is to allow an angle to occur where the supporting leg joins the body. This can be avoided if the hips are squarely placed directly over the supporting foot and the raised knee is well turned out.

7. The shoulders must not be pulled backwards. Rather, they should be widened from under the arms and pressed as far as possible away from the ears. This lengthens the neck and frees it from strain. Lifting the shoulders whilst turning is sometimes only habit, but a very difficult one to combat. It can be caused by lack of confidence in retaining the balance during the spin or by an involuntary wish to take the weight off a sore foot. (Pirouettes should never be practised on point if a shoe is not giving the foot sufficient support.)

8. The head must never incline but must be governed by the eyes remaining horizontal (i.e., when the head is tilted, one eye becomes further away from the floor than the other). The eyes remain focused on a point only so long as is comfortable. The head must then turn sharply to re-focus on the same spot. While anticipating the turn of the body, it remains level and steady until the body continues to complete the turn.

9. The arms should always remain in the given position for the entire pirouette. When this is fifth *en avant,* the space between the hands must be opposite the centre of the body and should not slip to the side. The height of the elbows and hands is a controversial point open to much argument, and I believe a certain laxity should be allowed a student in order that he may find his own natural turning position. For example, the arms pulled down in fifth *en bas* can look very effective but will not allow multiple pirouettes, due to the rigidity of the position. A girl making a supported turn must ensure that her elbows are above her partner's hands (which are controlling the turn on her waist) and that her wrists are crossed in front of her chest.

10. During the preparation, the front arm (slightly aided by the shoulder) should be allowed to overcross the centre line of the body, permitting a strong swing to give impetus and arriving square with the pelvis for the actual turn. The first arm must not be flung beyond the second position as this causes the shoulder to poke forward and dislocates the balance.

Of course the trick of turning is greatly helped by a natural 'knack' and lack of fear, but pirouettes can be acquired by diligence and strict adherence to all the rules with the emphasis on rhythmic co-ordination, correct placing and use of eyes. I say 'eyes' purposely in preference to 'head', as too much detailed explanation of movements in 'spotting' often leads to awkwardness and an over-consciousness of what the head is doing. So long as the eyes have time to focus properly on each return to the front, it is not necessary to jerk the head so quickly that the balance of the shoulders is upset.

Another feeling to be found is that of two simultaneous but contrary tensions in the body. In other words the 'spirit' of the pirouette starts in the feet and creates a definite current that runs up to the top of the scalp, whereas the physical feeling is heavy and must push down from the shoulders through the body and concentrate in the foot, where the whole weight is firmly upon the floor.

All turns need weight and breadth. One has only to spin a pencil and a coin to see which maintains its balance longer; and so it is obvious that a thin drawn-up feeling will not be as secure as one based solidly on the supporting foot.

Another difficulty is the amount of amalgamated strength and relaxation to be used. The best turns are easy and unforced while being nonetheless disciplined and controlled. No particular strength is needed to stand upright, nor is a stretched leg necessarily hard and muscular. Thus if a dancer is in the habit of working with well pulled up knees and a proper carriage of head and back, he will not require any extra strength to make a pirouette. In fact, in the last moment before the turn, the body and arms should be entirely free and relaxed, the swing of the opening arm should be wide and loose and not controlled in the shoulders (apart from not allowing it to swing too far); here the rhythmic co-ordination is to be found.

After the relaxed preparation to give impetus, it is the knack of making the *relevé* and pulling arms and legs quickly and firmly into a turning position at exactly the right moment, that gives a smooth spin.

The ability to teach and correct pirouettes is a particular talent in itself! It may be an advantage for the instructor to be able to turn well himself and understand from his own experience that peculiar ecstatic feeling of accomplishment after performing 'more turns' than usual, but this does not always go with the gift of observation and is not enough in itself. It can also cause psychological damage to a student whose only reaction to the sight of his teacher performing multiple pirouettes is disgust at his own attempts and a consequent feeling of hopelessness. I therefore believe that turns should not be demonstrated too often but should be coaxed along with encouragement and not overcorrected. The teacher must know by a trained and critical eye—or sometimes by a sixth sense—just exactly what small mistake has caused a turn to fall off balance. So often this is not a visible fault but rather a mistiming of co-ordination; therefore the trainer must not only watch what the student is doing but mentally pirouette with him and so sense in his own body where the trouble lies. He must also have a good understanding of the student's psychology. Some pupils will make three good pirouettes for the first time, simply by being told they are able to do so; others by being told they must. But most of them, when asked to make more turns than they have made hitherto, will fall over earlier than usual! (I speak here of students in the course of training and not of experienced dancers, though they too often have periods when their pirouettes suddenly disintegrate, and their balance is lost.) In all cases when a turn is not straight and secure, the dancer's confidence must be restored by stopping practice of the spin and refinding the equilibrium. This can be done by making a small *echappé sauté* into second or fourth position and immediately a *relevé* into the pirouette position, holding the balance on the half point for as long as possible. It is sometimes necessary to do this for several days before again attempting the turn.

I have dealt here only with upright, multiple pirouettes, though these are by no means the only way of turning. However, they are the best preparation for the head and arms and are a very necessary part of a contemporary dancer's equipment if he wants to achieve brilliance.

Here is a short *enchaînement* illustrating several points I have made in this chapter: To a slow 4/4 and travelling on the diagonal. (Music in 3/4 can also be used for this exercise.)

> Stand on the right leg, the left leg *degagé croisée derrière*
> *Coupé dessous* with a quarter turn to the right, (and)
> *Chassé en quatrième ouverte en avant* with the right arm *cinquième en avant,* (1)

One turn *en dedans* in the first arabesque, (and)

Fondu facing the travelling direction and swing the left leg quickly *à la seconde* (2)

Two *relevé pirouettes en dedans* working foot just under the knee, (and) Drop onto the left leg, right foot neatly *sur le cou de pied derrière* (3) *Pas de bourré dessous en tournant* with a small *renversé,* and ending with a *chassé en quatrième ouverte* (and er 4) Repeat on the same leg making the first *coupé, en tournant.*

When this *enchaînement* is well performed, it will be seen to possess a marked and interesting rhythmic phrasing. Each time the body revolves, a different speed and a different quality is called for. The first turn in arabesque is sustained and comparatively slow, without too sharp a head movement and with the upper body and shoulders slightly in front of the supporting foot. The following double (or triple) *relevé pirouette en dedans* should be at least twice as fast, very erect, and with a sharply marked spotting movement of the head. On the *tombé* before the *pas de bourré en tournant* the head should incline well over the shoulder and make a *renversé* movement similar to that of Spanish dancers, though more moderate, and finally, the *coupé en tournant* before recommencing the combination should be very rapid, leaving the audience unsure if the dancer has turned or not.

By this modest example of only four different speeds and qualities of turn, it will be seen that the human body can spin and revolve in all manner of moods. Pirouettes become a very exciting adornment to dancing when both dancers and choreographers understand they possess colour and expression of their own.

8. Batterie

Perhaps of all the advances made in classical ballet technique over the last hundred years *petite batterie* has made the least progress. At a time when the legs of a female dancer were so well covered by clothes that nothing of their shape could be seen, the work of the feet had an important part to play, and a great deal of time and energy was spent in perfecting their performance. The tight corseting of a woman actually changed her natural figure and the waist was literally squeezed away, upwards and downwards, enlarging the hips and the bosom. The ballerina of the nineteenth century was definitely rounded and under those ballet skirts was probably a pair of thighs the shape of which would not be tolerated today. But still those legs were a working pair of limbs which gave the dancer *ballon* and sparkle. How else could these dancers of a bygone age have inspired eulogies such as this?

'How she flies, how she rises, how she soars! How at home she is in the air! When, from time to time, the tip of her little foot skims the ground, it is easy to see that it is out of pure good nature, so as not to drive those who have no wings to despair.' (Théophile Gautier)

It was considered essential to give this illusion of weightlessness or flying, and the dancers must have had extraordinary strength. Studying contemporary prints, one can only come to the conclusion that the necessary thigh and calf muscles were developed expressly for this and without too much consideration for visual aesthetics.

But ideals are different now, and although dancers of today admire these qualities, very few of them can give satisfactory performances of the romantic ballets. Perhaps we should blame abstract works performed in 'all-over' tights for this. In these ballets a dancer's body should have no lumps or bumps, no overdeveloped muscles or superfluous flesh. It must be perfect and youthful, revealing itself in every line and movement as an instrument, almost sexless, devoted to pattern and to the service of the choreographer. This body should evoke an abstract emotion far removed from sentiment. It should be nude in the sence of graphic art, not naked meaning undressed. This ideal is quite different from the still-prevalent conception of ballet being twinkle toes and pink.

The technique demanded in these modern ballets is a formidable combination of strength, acrobatics and cool control. The *pointes* must be steely, the extensions very high and in most cases, where difficult *pas de deux* are involved, there must be 'guts'.

This may seem irrelevant to a chapter on *petite batterie* and is certainly far removed from the romantic ballet. Nevertheless, it demonstrates the increasing demands faced by today's students and the difficulties of creating dancers capable of all styles. I am referring here to girls, since although overdeveloped thigh muscles are for men also '*démodé*', *batterie* is not quite such a lost art to male dancers. The problem is to achieve speed in the feet and retain the long athletic limbs in accordance with today's precepts of beauty.

Even if our ideas now differ from those of the Romantic era, we can still learn a lot by examining the methods of the nineteenth century teachers and trying to emulate their discipline and exactitude. It is surely still true to say that a ballerina placing her foot with fastidious care upon the floor lends aristocratic qualities to a step, and this attention to detail need in no way curb a dancer's range. On the contrary, it adds distinction to movements and indirectly refines the muscles. So *petite batterie,* practised with care and moderation, should help the feet to gain precision and elegance.

A clear division should be apparent between *petite batterie* and *grands sauts,* just as there should always be a marked difference between *ballon* and elevation, which are by no means similar qualities. Whereas the important factor in large jumps is to spring high and defy gravity, small beats should accentuate the closings, using the floor as a small drum and bouncing from it quite evenly but not high. (See illustration p. 98.) In the category of *petite batterie* one must include beaten *jetés* and *assemblés,* all *brisés, royales, entrechats trois, quatre, cinq,* and *small cabrioles,* etc. *Entrechat huit, entrechats de volées* and double *cabrioles* all belong to *grands sauts. Entrechat six* really belongs to both groups, but only an advanced student can manage it in the rhythm of *petite batterie.*

Beats should only be taught when the student has developed strong and supple feet, control in the turn-out of the knee, both in stretching and in *demi plié,* and sufficient strength in the back and legs to enable him to perform a series of *temps levés* without straining the neck or letting the body collapse during the *demi plié.*

It is best to start by practising *échappé sauté à la seconde* closing *battu.* When the legs can bounce freely together, just below the calf, before changing, one can start jumping from fifth before the beat. Some people follow with *changement battu,* but a beginner will sometimes draw the legs together with contracted tension immediately on leaving the floor, and I therefore prefer to teach *entrechat quatre* next, where the legs are forced to part in order to change before the beat. If the feet leave the ground with a strong final push from the toes, the legs will already be sufficiently apart to change and beat without a further movement of separation. (See illustration p. 90.) At the moment of beating both legs should be fully extended with a strong feeling of turn-out pushing the inside of the limb, from thigh to heel, well forward. The teacher must understand anatomically the structure of the leg to be corrected. Dancers with sway-back knees will have real trouble crossing the feet for the beat if the legs are hyper-extended; and they must be told to bend the knees very slightly, but not to relax them. On the other hand, pupils with a tendency to bandy legs can usually beat with little trouble. However, to give a brilliant effect, legs of this type should be well extended towards the floor in order to avoid shortening and spoiling the line by pulling the feet up under the body.

All *batterie* is more impressive when exact and fast. It is essential that the whole body is alive, neither tensed nor totally relaxed, but holding unseen power in reserve. Brilliance comes through effortless work; and this is only possible with good placing and fast, tidy footwork. A large slow jump should never be taken before a beaten step, as this sort of preparation looks sluggish and does not exercise the legs for speed.

In small *brisés* and *jetés battus* it is important to keep the weight of the shoulders forward, and endeavour to beat with the feet also slightly in front of the line of the body (except of course in steps travelling *en arrière*). When the heels are really pressed forward in the air, this will happen naturally and it should not be contrived by letting the posterior sit out. A student brushing the preparation leg directly to the side for a *brisé dessus* will find the supporting leg has to travel backwards to beat it, sometimes causing the knees to fall forward and the shoulders to jerk in order to counteract the balance. Correctly, the first leg should extend slightly in front of the supporting foot, with the turn-out well controlled in the pelvis. Likewise in a *brisé dessous,* the working leg makes a very slight *rond de jambe en dehors,* so that both heels are pressed forward during the beat and the first leg does not drop in or cause a wriggle in the hips.

A common fault in *brisés* is to see the preparation leg extend quite high before the push off from the supporting foot. This means that the first leg will be descending before the beat is made. I think it is always advantageous to teach children to stretch both knees at the same time, after allowing the first foot to slide out of the fifth position during the downward thrust of the *plié,* otherwise a nasty habit of performing the step in two movements will creep in.

A Mazurka is a good rhythm for practice, and here is an elementary exercise for teaching *brisés.*

Place both hands on the barre; stand in fifth position and make a *demi plié,* (and)
Now execute a *brisé dessus* quite sharply, travelling in the direction of the first leg and making sure the feet land in the fifth position simultaneously, (1)
Stretch the knees while strongly controlling the fifth position, (2)
Repeat the *demi plié,* taking care the feet do not slip into a turned-in position before the preparation, (3)
Repeat the *brisé* twice in the same direction and then execute a *changement* in the same rhythm.
Repeat the *enchaînement,* starting with the other foot.

Children should not be allowed to press on the *barre* during this exercise, though it is permissible to take a little weight on the hands in order that the *brisé* may be properly beaten. Having both hands on the *barre* is a method of keeping the body square and care should be taken that the hips are not displaced. As with *brisé,* so with *cabriole;* the supporting leg must rise to join the first leg, the beat taking place between ankle and calf muscle, as in all *petite batterie.* All the previously discussed rules apply here; and again the dancer must guard against cramping the legs together with too much tension at the time of the beat, since this will prevent the execution of a double *cabriole.*

Generally, all beaten steps should begin with a strong, fast, and forceful push from the ground, and the beats should occur at the highest point. It is a fault, however, to wait till the top of the jump in *entrechat six* and *huit* before changing the legs, as this causes a hurried scraping of the feet on the way down and can result in injuries through incorrect landing. The contrary should take place. The beats must occur as late as possible on the way up, and with particular attention to 'turn-out'.

In fact nowhere is 'turn-out' more important than in *petite batterie.*

It is impossible for the heels to cross neatly one in front of the other when the knees are pointing forward. This is where the dangers of an acrobatic and over-forced 'turn-out' become apparent. The student can probably perform loose and well placed *grands battements* or even *développés,* but has no control over the actual turn of the leg in the hip socket, especially during movements requiring rapid tension in the inside of the leg or lower back.

'Turn-out' is something a dancer does, not necessarily something he has.

An excellent and traditional *enchaînement* for perfecting these exciting and sparkling steps is *petite brisé en tournant,* and probably comes to us from Bournonville via the Danish School. This is first taught without the turn and with a short pause between each jump. Later, when each beat has a sharp dry finish, it is done more rapidly and finally with a quarter turn on each jump.

Stand on the right foot, *en fondu,* left foot *sur le cou de pied devant* and flexed.
Brisé en avant from one foot to the same foot, (and 1)
Jeté battu derrière, (and 2)
Brisé en arrière from one foot to the same foot, (and 3)
Jeté battu devant (and 4)

When turning (using the Cecchetti corner numbering), the step commences in corner 3 and travels in a diagonal line to corner 1. The body is facing 1, and after the first *brisé,* faces 4. On the next *jeté* it faces 3, on the next *brisé,* 2, and on the last *jeté,* ends facing 1. The left arm is brought well across the body en *cinquième en avant*, and the head is left over the left shoulder on the first two steps, turns sharply on the third and is over the right shoulder on the fourth step, the right arm now being *cinquième en avant,* left arm *à la seconde*.

In general, good *batterie* can best be achieved by thorough preparation of the feet and knees. Plenty of short controlled *battements glissés* at the *barre* with a strongly arched foot and accentuated closing are good; they exercise the Achilles tendon well and should be given daily. Also important is the correct warm-up in the centre. That is to say, before the small beaten steps of allegro, a dancer must be given simple jumps, taking off and landing on two feet and must never be expected to jump fast while cold or before the *barre* work is completed.

Though it is usually the muscular dancer with shortish tendons and often little instep who can beat easily from the beginning, I see no reason why, with proper training, the bodies of longer and looser dancers cannot be sufficiently strengthened and quickened to enable them also to command this brilliant technical work. Surely Markova gave us a supreme example of the lightness and speed which beautiful feet can achieve, and how could anyone who saw her as Giselle forget the excitement and beauty of her *entrechats* in the second act of this ballet?

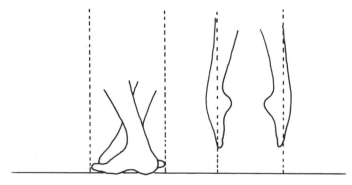

This illustration demonstrates how the dancer should leave the ground with a healthy push, employing all the muscles in the foot to stretch the instep and toes; the legs should neither pull towards each other nor make an extra separating movement.

9. Elevation

Jumping is a built-in human faculty. To give only three examples: it occurs as a safety valve for excessive high spirits in children, as a natural expression of rhythm in most folklore dancing or just as a self-preservation reflex action.

If it is so much part of our physical equipment, it follows that at all stages of training a student's natural *ballon* should be exercised and preserved. It is often found that people well endowed with this quality have a highly developed sense of rhythm and this is the key to all unstrained and soaring springs. In fact I believe jumping is 50 per cent rhythmic co-ordination, 25 per cent technique and strength, and 25 per cent temperament and joy. To sustain a jump is momentarily to become immortal, an instant defying gravity. At the top of the spring the breath is held, the body is taut and lifted, and one resists the downward fall by 'willing' to stop in the air. Call this what you will—imagination, sensuality, animal spirits—it is a gift of temperament that lies in the individual and cannot be taught but can be helped by developing the mechanism, e.g. muscles, and teaching the dancer how to divide and use his energy.

Analysis in ballet can be destructive in that it takes apart and renders in words and theories something that exists in another medium. Therefore only analysis which concerns itself with technique can be constructive and even if, as in this case, one can deal with only 25 per cent of the problem, it still offers more help than lofty theorizing. This, in a way, proves that the best jumps are all born and given control while still on the ground.

When leaping, a large number of muscles are brought into play, and together these have a natural rhythm of their own which will respond to musical tempi. An untrained child, told to skip to music, will automatically try to jump higher as the tempo becomes slower. It is the duty of training and technique to assist this automatic reaction by providing deep and soft *plié* and strong feet, legs and back but not to interfere with the co-ordination of push and pull taking place rhythmically in the body. It is the fault of bad training if a young dancer becomes earthbound, due either to over turning out the feet—thereby weakening the knees—or to over loosening the legs in the hip sockets and causing a lack of 'grip' in the lower back.

When the quality of natural *ballon* is observed, it will be seen to have an even rhythm—a high spring requiring a deeper *plié*, and a small spring a short 'dry' *plié*. (See illustration p. 98.) Just as a diver makes a heavy downward push on the springboard before soaring upward, so must a dancer use the floor to initiate his spring. After the final contact with the floor nothing can help other than the breath and the 'will'. Therefore, all the work should take place in the energetic push out of the *plié* before the jump, and on leaving the ground, the impetus of the rising body will pull the legs with it. Watch any animal spring and notice how grace in the air is achieved through a release from the initial contraction.

On landing, one should reach for the floor and settle slowly like a big bird: feet, knees, pelvis, ribs, arms. So long as the shoulders do not fall forwards, I believe there is no harm in letting the body crunch together a little between jumps, as this is equivalent to the action of a coiled wire spring and gives dramatic effect and phrasing to leaps. When an elegant *ballon* or appearance of complete ease is aimed at, then of course the chest should be held lifted during the *plié* and the work completely hidden in the thighs and the base of the spine.

It is dangerous however to overemphasize the importance of this *plié* since, when it becomes lower or slower than the height of the spring demands, it has the reverse effect, the muscles becoming heavy and losing elasticity. The student should not be allowed to 'sit' in a *plié* after a jump but must immediately stretch the knees or rebound into a further spring. (It can be beneficial, however, for advanced male students to pause in *plié* between small jumps, as this greatly strengthens the thigh muscles.) Some dancers, when pushing off, leave the floor at an incorrect angle, usually because either the pelvis has been misplaced, or one foot has given more impetus than the other. They then try to adjust themselves in the air by waving their arms about and land tensely. They should rather think of the direction of the spring before taking off and imagine the aerial curve to be made. As Johansson said, 'Look with your feet and not with your eyes.'

The relative length of limbs also plays a large part in the ability to jump high. One often notices that boys with a short compact build will have an advantage over the longer-limbed type. However there are some famous exceptions, and surely everything depends on developing the right muscles and co-ordination.

A great jumper—the frog—has very long legs when they are outstretched, giving him all the more push off. (One wonders how long are the legs of a flea!) It is interesting to note, however, that races living in mountain districts definitely tend to have shorter legs than those from the plains. As the modern *danseur noble* (I do not speak here of character dancers) tends to grow longer, I can only recommend that boys of this physical type should not spend too much time on developing line and lyric qualities, which usually come easily to them but concentrate on steps of strength and bravura.

Good jumps are essential for male dancers and nearly every boy's solo variation is a display of strength and technique. It is therefore not surprising, though it is certainly disturbing, that the poor overworked knee joint and Achilles tendon are prone to injury and are a very common source of trouble. The best insurance against these injuries, which nearly always occur when landing, is conscientious preliminary training and proper understanding of the function of the knees in *demi plié*. Only when this has been mastered should one concentrate on increasing the elevation.

The action and importance of the foot can be demonstrated quite simply as follows:

Place the right hand flat against a wall, bending the elbow, and leaning with all the weight of the body upon it. Now push away sharply and observe how the base of the palm pushes on the wall and, as the elbow stretches, peels away with a final push from the fingers. The feet should work likewise, supposing the base of the palm to be the heel; the fingers, the toes; and the elbow, the knee.

This push from the heel is often handicapped by short tendons behind the ankle (the Achilles) preventing the student making a deep *plié* without raising the heels, and in some cases causing him to contract the instep muscles on landing. This reduces the efficiency of the foot and sometimes causes cramp and muscle pains in the front of the ankle or shin. The only remedy is gently and systematically to lengthen, or more accurately 'relax', the Achilles tendon.

For a strong push from the toes one needs a well developed and flexible instep, and this is best exercised by slow *battements tendus*. The whole foot must be well pushed down and relaxed in the fifth position. As the leg moves to the open position, keep the heel down as long as possible, then lift it firmly, passing through the *demi-pointe* and finishing with it as high as possible from the floor but with the pointed toes *à terre*. The heel must never be allowed to push forward, flexing and weakening the foot, or backwards, thereby 'sickling'.

When a beginner is learning *assemblé,* it is not wise to give him a series following one after the other. A stop should be made between each to ensure that the fifth position is good and the heels are on the ground. Land in *demi plié en cinquième,* stretch the knees and then *plié* again as preparation for the next *assemblé*.

A fault often found in beginners' *assemblés* is too large a *battement* with the first foot, and too little spring off the second. This is sometimes caused by dividing the movement into two parts: one, Brush out, two, Spring and close fifth. This is incorrect, as the extension should assist and be part of the spring, and the accent should be on the closing (and *one*). This fault can also be caused by sliding out the first leg with a straight knee, while the supporting leg makes a *fondu*. It gives the jump a lop-sided appearance and throws unnecessary strain on the second leg. The definition of *assemblé* is a jump from one leg landing on two. Therefore, if the step starts from fifth, the *demi plié* and sliding out of the working leg—heel pushed as long as possible on the ground—is all preparation. The step itself consists of a strong push into the air from the supporting leg *at the same time as the battement,* the bringing together of the legs at the height of the jump (sometimes with slightly bent knees) and descent in the fifth position. Bending the knees in the air is the old method of *assemblé* and was practised in the Italian School. It strengthens the inside thigh muscles and encourages students to work with the feet forward and knees back. The 'split' *assemblé,* so often seen nowadays, where the legs separate at the height of the jump, is exciting only when combined with a high elevation and should be confined to *assemblé porté*.

The position of the arms at the apex of the spring can make or mar the entire effect of any jump. First, they must not lag behind the action of the feet but anticipate the movement, helping a dancer by co-ordinating the take-off and by appearing to be an extension of the filling of the lungs. Secondly, they must be in place during the climax of the spring and float after the body on the return to the ground. This is achieved entirely by strength in the upper back, behind and slightly below the armpits. I cannot stress too strongly how important it is to cultivate an awareness of this part of the body. Breathing is clearly also a fundamental part of jumping, and to illustrate my point let me suggest a small test. Stand with the elbows pressed against the ribs, meanwhile making short, shallow respirations, and it will be found to be physically impossible to make a large spring while doing this. Therefore, while performing steps of *grand sauté* let the body and arms expand as though filling with air and avoid contracting movements at all costs. Stiff arms, strained necks or faulty rhythm can often be attributed to inadequate breathing technique.

Perhaps it helps a dancer to imagine he is jumping through thick cloud and that at the top his head bursts through into sunshine and he takes a look around for as long as possible. This also helps him to sustain and enjoy the position at the top! So it will be seen the execution of *grand sauté* and steps of virtuosity consists simply of the application of strength to basic fundamental technique. The pleasing performance of these steps, however, (apart from the obvious necessity for the above mechanics) relies largely on the musical sense of the dancer and the expressive use of arms, head and face.

All point and purpose of the preparatory years of training are lost when in the

actual performance the technique is too obvious. The very essence of jumping is ease and lightness.

I would like to illustrate a fairly elementary *sauté enchaînement* suitable for girls and boys, paying particular attention to directions and arms.

> Travelling on the diagonal. Start fifth position *en face*. Left foot front. Left arm raised *cinquième en haut*. Right arm low *à la seconde,* the head slightly forward looking under the left arm.
>
> Music 2/4.
>
> *Assemblé dessus,* changing direction to finish *croisé* with the right foot front *en cinquième, demi plié.*
>
> Arms open through second finish *en bas* (and 1,2,)
>
> *Sissonne ouverte* to the first arabesque on right foot, travelling in direction of diagonal (*2,2,*)
>
> *Temps levé* on right foot, opening the right arm to second (and)
>
> *Chassé passé croisé* with the left foot. Left arm fifth *en avant,* bring the right foot *sur le cou de pied derrière* and place in fifth, (*3,2,*)
>
> *Assemblé en avant croisé* taking the left arm up to fifth *en haut* and looking under it, (*4,2,*)

This exercise can be done to a 3/4 rhythm, jumping slower and higher. In this case the last *assemblé* should be *porté* with the legs carried well forward and held together.

The most infectious springs are those with gaiety, the most dramatic those with purpose. Dancers should think of their elevation as a means of creating special moods or effects rather than as individual steps of virtuosity, for in this way gravity can be defied more successfully.

Many people dream they are flying or are suspended weightlessly and some dancers develop their dreams in this category to find themselves effortlessly executing *entrechat vingt-quatre* or five *tours en l'air*. Psychiatrists may explain it as they will, but man's natural desire to conquer gravity has taken us to the moon; and in their own context, the attempts of dancers are no less valid.

Diagram showing the different qualities of spring. The horizontal
line represents the floor: below this the undulating line indicates the depth
and duration of the *plié,* and above it the height and duration of the jump.

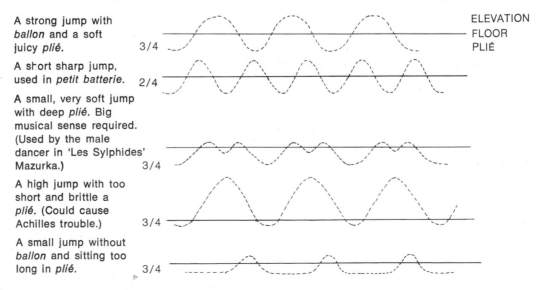

A strong jump with *ballon* and a soft juicy *plié.*　3/4

A short sharp jump, used in *petit batterie.*　2/4

A small, very soft jump with deep *plié.* Big musical sense required. (Used by the male dancer in 'Les Sylphides' Mazurka.)　3/4

A high jump with too short and brittle a *plié.* (Could cause Achilles trouble.)　3/4

A small jump without *ballon* and sitting too long in *plié.*　3/4

ELEVATION
FLOOR
PLIÉ

10. 'Pointe' Work

If Taglioni were to return to earth and make a quick tour of the ballet schools of the world, she would surely regard the repercussions of her flights on to point in the interests of romantic illusion with astonishment and perhaps regret. Can we really hold her responsible for the grotesque exhibition of children dislocating their toe joints in the worship of Terpsichore, or have we so deformed her motives for dancing on her 'toes' that comparison is absurd? Of course she was not alone, as the many romanticized engravings of other dancers of this period show us, nor, it is thought, was she the first to rise on point; but her name will always be remembered because of the many descriptions of her: 'She floats like a blush of light before our eyes: we cannot perceive the subtle means by which she contrives, as it were, to disdain the earth, and to deliberate her charming motions in the air. She achieves the office of wings without their encumbrance.' At all events *La Dance sur les pointes* arrived during the first half of the nineteenth century and has been entrenching itself ever since.

Periodically, great lone figures pioneering a new path have rocked the establishment, but they have only succeeded in airing the hothouse conservatories of classical ballet without fundamentally changing the 'modern' dancer's bête noir, the Point Shoe. A few names that jump to mind, Duncan, St. Denis, Wigman, Laban and Jooss, all started schools of 'free dance' and were in essence a manifestation of their time and style. But point work remained in spite of passing fashions, and, having survived isolated decades of degeneration in various lands, is still with us, perhaps less abused than formerly and an enrichment of the vocabulary of classical ballet.

The aesthetic advantages are not difficult to recognize: they are the elongated line of leg, the illusion of weightlessness, the negation of 'feet' with all the connotations of 'feet of clay' or 'feet firmly planted'. There are also practical assets, such as less resistance to the floor in pirouettes; refinement of the calf muscle by having the weight of the body directly over the supporting toes, rather than slightly behind, which is the case when standing on *demi pointe;* and the necessary strengthening of the foot which takes place whilst training to stand on point and which helps efficiency in other steps.

Nearly all experienced dancers prefer working on point, whether in class, rehearsal or performance since, once the discipline is mastered and has become automatic, it is less tiring.

Many contemporary choreographers use point work as part of the natural raw material of the female dancers with whom they work and I think this is as it should be. Of course when it creates a discrepancy with the style of the ballet, it should be discarded, but not despised.

The wearing of a tu-tu in classical ballet is unthinkable without the aristocratic, refined foot of the ballerina *sur les pointes*. Likewise, many abstract and symphonic ballets, where an uninterrupted line is desirable, could give a very proletarian effect if danced on half point. Surely the degree of point work used today depends on costume, style, and the requirements of the choreographer.

The year at which a child should begin point work is a matter of controversy. Because so much depends upon the physique of the pupil, the standard of her technique, and the rate of progress, it is impossible to categorically state an age. In ideal circumstances, a child receiving regular training (at least three lessons a week) from the age of eight should after four years have developed the necessary muscles

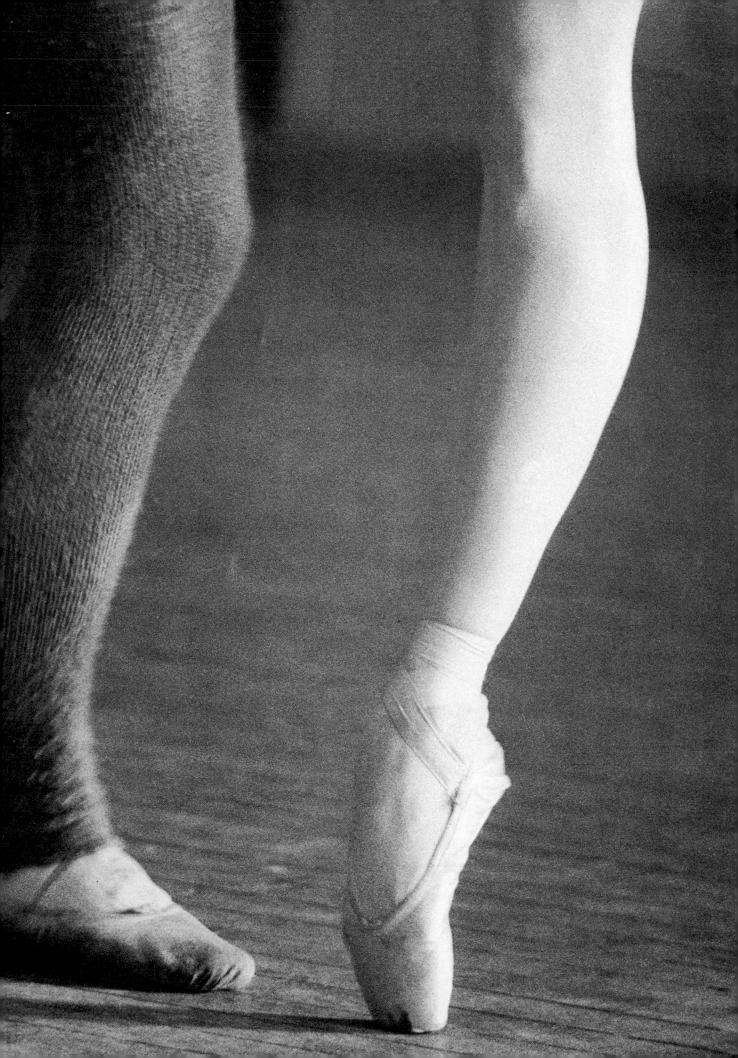

in her legs and body to stand on point without danger to her feet; but it is extremely unwise for children under fourteen years of age to work in point shoes with less preparation than this. So often one sees small pupils, aged perhaps seven or eight, whose ambition—or whose mother's ambition—has persuaded the teacher to 'let them try'; they have perhaps silenced the doubts by managing extremely well and have convinced everyone they are baby ballerinas. The results are often tragic. The too-soft bones of the feet become dislocated because muscles to deal with the lifting of the weight of the body on to the toes are not yet sufficiently developed to protect them; as the children grow older and heavier, bad cases of malformation can occur, so that a dancing career is ruined before it has begun.

When possible, children wishing to train as professionals should be chosen with great care and with special attention paid to the structure of the foot. Whereas some children without a natural instep can develop a passable and often very serviceable foot, there are certain bone formations which can never be altered enough to allow the foot to arch sufficiently below the stretched knee and constantly spoil the work by bad line. These sad cases could be avoided if parents were honestly informed of the risk at the beginning of a child's training. An ideal foot, before training, should be supple enough to pass this simple test: Make the child sit on the floor with her legs stretched out in front, the backs of the knees touching the floor if possible. Now, keeping the knees taut, arch the foot, forcing the big toe joint (not necessarily the toes) down towards the floor. If the ball of the foot can reach a point nearer the floor than the ankle bone, the foot is sufficiently arched.

Good foot.   Insufficient arch.

The human foot varies amazingly from one person to another; and it is unwise—indeed almost impossible—to lay down rigid rules for training. Each foot needs individual care, and this is where a teacher with much experience, and preferably many years of dancing herself, has an advantage. Quite often a very beautiful foot (meaning one with a large instep) is extremely weak and needs special attention. For example, a beginner making a highly arched *battement tendu* is likely to develop a roll forward unless power and control are given to the foot through intensive strengthening exercises. Conversely, an obstinate foot needs first to be made supple, rather than to be admonished constantly to 'point'. Students with little arch often have extremely 'tough' feet and, when in *demi plié*, can hop on point quite easily; but when the leg is straight and upright, and the foot has insufficient arch for the toes to arrive beneath the weight of the body, the student must either fall back off her point or hold herself there by sheer strength, which will result in large and unsightly calf muscles. So it is apparent that with only two types of foot falling short of perfection, two different and specialized approaches to training are necessary.

It is an advantage when the toes are not too long, the first three being smoothly graded in length from the big toe. If the second is longer than the first, it often bends when in a point shoe and the upstanding knuckle becomes badly blistered. When standing *sur les pointes* the toes should never curl under so that the weight of the

102

body rests upon the joints. This is extremely damaging and can sometimes occur when a child's first point shoes are too large and do not hold the foot (the toes in particular) firmly together. (See illustration below.) Slippers stiffened and strengthened by darning have been replaced by a modern shoe made of composite materials and the traditional satin, hardened with glue and built to support the foot strongly without interfering with flexibility. During *adage* and multiple pirouettes the dancers of today can remain on one point for a quite considerable time, something out of the question a hundred years ago.

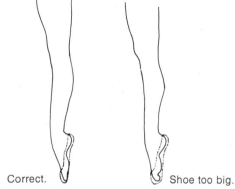

Correct.   Shoe too big.

For a normal healthy foot I find it nearly always an advantage to work in softish point shoes, so that the foot itself becomes accustomed to taking the weight of the body. With very hard shoes one comes to rely too much on their support, and their rigidity prevents supple movements of the feet, often allowing only two positions: on the flat foot and on the full point with no intermediary control. Also, and worst of all, the shoes can be heard, thereby destroying all possible illusion. Taglioni's father is known to have said that the day he 'heard' his daughter on the stage he would disown her. Great care should be taken concerning the fit and suitability of shoes. A dancer's feet are too valuable to be made to suffer through ignorance or abused in any way under the impression that blisters and painful feet are all part of the necessary toughening up process. On the other hand, point work is no way harmful when approached sensibly. In fact, it should be the inevitable result of strongly stretched feet. It is not particularly clever, and certainly not beautiful, when performed as an endurance stunt. As already stated, a well prepared student will find the majority of steps easier on full point than on half point, and, when accustomed to working consistently in point shoes, will also find that the slightly stricter discipline required, for example in knees, back and pelvis, prevents slipshod execution. The majority of accidents to knees, feet and ankles occur in unguarded moments when one is not paying due attention to small details.

It must not be thought that dancing on point is always preferable to half point, and the dancer must try to combine the best qualities of both in her work. By this I mean the softness of imperceptible rises and *fondu*, usually associated with work on half point, can be achieved on point with strong feet, and the disciplinary turn out and stretched legs of dancing *sur les pointes* should equally benefit work on *demi pointe*.

The main difference, most apparent in insufficiently trained dancers, is in the *relevé*. Any elementary pupil can stand on one foot and rise smoothly on to the half point, the ball of the foot remaining stationary. However, to do this on point the stu-

dent must make first a *demi plié* and then a slight spring, simultaneously stretching the knee and drawing the pointed toe a little backwards to arrive under the weight of the body. This can give a jerky appearance if not correctly executed, and, when accompanied by heaving shoulders and an expression of achievement or surprise on arrival, is a performance tolerated only by doting mothers.

A good *en dehors* position of the foot is controlled entirely by the turn out of the leg in the hip socket. This is easily checked by seeing if the heels slip back while the feet are on point in the second position. To make a pupil conscious of the correct muscles to be employed she should be placed facing the *barre,* both hands resting lightly upon it, the feet *à la seconde* turned in and parallel to each other. Make a small *demi plié,* and *relevé* on both feet, knees stretched and facing forward. Now turn the legs outwards in the hip sockets till the tightly pulled up knees are facing sideways and note how the muscles in the base of the spine contract, whereas those inside the thighs press forward. Remain for two counts, then slowly come down through the half point, pressing the heels forward and leaving the knees stretched. Now *relevé* four times with the feet *à la seconde* and with a well turned out *demi plié* between each.

When a student makes a habit of using maximum turn out while on point and during the *demi plié* before and after a *relevé,* she will observe how much more secure all balances and pirouettes become.

Practise the following *enchaînement* for control in front of a mirror. Commencing at the back of the room, arms *à la seconde.*

> *Piqué en avant en arabesque, en face,* (1) (The supporting heel should be well visible and the working leg hidden behind the body.)
> Make a firm *demi plié* on the supporting leg, holding the other tightly *en arabesque,* (and)
> *Relevé* in this postion twice, the last time raising the arms to *cinquìeme en haut* and holding the balance, (2, and 3, 4)
> *Fondu* bringing the lifted leg neatly *sur le cou de pied en arrière* and make a *petit battement* before repeating the exercise on the other leg.
> Arms *en bas* (and)

As a general rule it is worthwhile to pay detailed attention to the feet when *en l'air,* so that eventually, from force of habit, the foot comes automatically into a strongly arched position as soon as it leaves the floor.

There is really no better preparation than this, as it means that at all times the foot is ready to step on point, and no extra strength or thought is suddenly required.

In these days of athletic technique, naturally much is called for, and, with the help of modern ballet shoes a dancer can stand on one point for a considerable time, but I would like to stress again how important it is not to forget the original reason, discussed at the beginning of this chapter, for rising upon the toes.

11. Mime

Mime, in the traditional sense, has become an almost forgotten art. Perhaps because of the intimate close-up technique of television and films and the fact that a producer can more fully exploit this medium by juxtaposing pictures to tell his story, larger than life histrionics have become outmoded. Nevertheless, on the rare stage occasions when one is confronted with human emotion portrayed in the grand manner, the impact is colossal.

Although television in England has destroyed Variety in the music hall and can be blamed for the closure of many theatres in the provinces, drama, opera, and ballet still survive and show no signs of extinction, however fluctuating their respective states of health. In Germany more opera houses exist per capita and bigger subsidies are given to the performing arts than in any other West European country, and a strong musical tradition prevails. Both in Eastern Europe and in North America, music, opera, and ballet flourish with great vigour. Surely all this means that no mechanical reproduction will ever be a satisfactory substitute for 'live' performance, and high drama must take pride of place where human dignity exists.

If we respect mankind and believe that to suffer and to show compassion, joy or generosity is ennobling, then we should recognize these things as riches; for when life is dulled by apathy or fear, existence becomes impoverished and meaningless. An intellectual culture without love is spiritually barren, and art without emotion is sterile.

Today all countries use their cultural inheritance, as embodied in music and the arts, to back up their diplomacy. So long as this remains non-political there is no better method for nations to communicate. On reflection, are not mime and dancing, of all theatrical arts, the most ancient and, metaphorically speaking, the most articulate? When confronted by strangers speaking an unknown foreign language does not everyone communicate by mime and gestures, and do not visiting dance companies from distant lands poetically convey to us more about their countries than if they were to try to say it in words? The paradox and perhaps tragedy of our time is that where mechanical means of transmitting news and information have reached the greatest efficiency through radio and television, the main social problem is still lack of communication between individuals. If we should lose the gift of mimicry, or expression through movement, we should be rendered even less articulate than we are already.

A present tendency in ballet towards producing only dehydrated abstract works could lead to stagnation, and I believe this should be countered by injections of robust drama. This is not to say all ballets without theme stagnate. On the contrary, the greatest beauty lies in simplicity or stripping an idea down to its bare essentials. Some abstract ballets do exactly this and succeed magnificently, but a clear division should be made between inspired works and barren posturing, which is humbug and far removed from valid art.

The pure imagination of young children playing 'pretend games' sometimes withers around the age of fourteen and is replaced by the self-conscious gaucheness of teenage behaviour. It is a pity that this so often destroys the joy of mimicry and make-believe that can, and should, continue into adult life. Is it also because too much canned entertainment dulls the need for children to create their own worlds of fantasy? Perhaps our scientific age reduces dreams to such a negligible stature that they are considered to be unproductive escapes for the naïve or as belonging to the realm

of dropouts. If this is really so, we are lost as individuals. However, as long as art flourishes I think there is still hope for us!

Certainly the wish for heightened experience is so strong that more and more young people are turning to drugs to induce these psychedelic flights. I believe that if the imagination were given more rein in schools and not artificially fostered in self-conscious 'Art' classes, where children are suddenly expected for one hour a week to 'express themselves', it would help adolescents to achieve a balanced maturity. By 'balanced,' I mean that every being should have a place in his psyche for reality and dreams, for accepting and living through the tragedies of life, and for human charity and enthusiasm. Surely ballet teachers have a mission to avoid producing the super technical machines now being cultivated for international sport and to place a little belief in mystery.

All this may seem irrelevant to a chapter on mime but is in essence a plea for its reinstatement in professional schools. I do not include in this plea the many schools for younger children, where I know invaluable work is still taking place. It is addressed to the establishments training students for careers in the ballet where too much time is spent on the mechanics of technique. Nothing is more exciting or lends more weight to a ballet, than to see mature artists, perhaps past their active dancing days, filling the stage with their presence in sometimes only minor acting roles. The Russians are particularly rich in these company members and use them to a degree which we should emulate.

The traditional mime of classical ballets is a very special art, fast becoming lost to us due to misuse and neglect. Like the great tradition of ballet itself, its technique can only be passed on by those in direct pedagogic lineage. Any reader who has seen Karsavina give a mime class will know what I mean. The formalized gestures, so easily learnt from textbooks, are quite meaningless when not accompanied by the right facial expression, the right phrasing, stance and quality. Therefore only the greatest attention to detail and belief in the meaning of the movements can recreate the genuine style. To say 'I saw a handsome man out hunting' is not difficult if the gesture for each word is understood, but as naïve narrative in ballet, this can become very tedious when not performed in an inspired fashion, and I think this is why traditional mime and gesture are so often dropped from new productions of classical ballets. However, it would be a genuine loss if it should disappear beyond recall, and I think schools should take steps to preserve this subject by including it in mime classes as a part of the heritage of ballet.

Marcel Marceau has shown us what mime can achieve when a great artist possesses acute observation. Whereas the mime of old ballets interrupted the dance action in order to relate the story, modern mime speaks to the audience by means of the actor or dancer becoming the character he wishes to convey, and this purer form should be taught alongside the stylized mime evolved in ballets during the last two hundred years.

In children's mime classes fifteen minutes or so should always be devoted to making nonexistent objects become visible. If, for example, the exercise is to open a door with a key, one must see what sort of key ring is taken out of the pocket, and, when it is returned, the pocket must be in exactly the same place. Another exercise is depicting weight. Not only do the body and limbs vary according to mood, but they must show that imaginary material things also have substance. A good exercise is to

pass four objects from one side to the other. The first should be a feather, the second a brick, the third a bucket full of water, and the fourth a large stone almost too heavy to lift. These exercises can be varied endlessly. A good mime should also be able to create figures and characters all around him. Let a child see an imaginary individual and go to greet him. The other pupils in the class must be able to guess what sort of a person he met and the relationship between the two.

Of course the face plays a role in all exercises similar to these, but it is the whole body that should be employed to convey the story to the audience, and for dancers this particular branch of mime is invaluable. For example, if in the mime class a given episode is to be enacted, the pupil must first decide upon his own character. (This governs stance, walk, facial expression, indication of the clothes he is wearing, state of mind, and any other characteristic traits that can be shown to establish a personality.) Secondly, by his gestures, reactions, and general floor pattern he should be able to furnish the stage with imaginary props and people. Finally he must decide upon a sequence of events and then go through them so as to wring every drop of understanding and self association out of his audience. This type of mime can be labelled practical and physical. Another type encroaches upon the domain of straight acting and is emotional. A student should believe himself in a given psychological state, and without facial expression (or with as little as possible) start to emanate this mood. When successful he will find that his whole body has played a part in the mental tensions, and this, when combined with dancing, is what gives that peculiar quality to great dramatic *pas de deux* when performed by sensitive dancers.

Of course belief is everything, and I am amazed how far the science of controlling and utilizing the enormous power of the mind lags behind other modern research. Transference of thought and hypnosis are still not yet conscious exercises for civilized minds, but the fact of their existence has long been recognized by scientists. Applying this to mime, a good example is that of a fat and rather ugly old teacher who played a memorable part as a dragon in my childhood. This woman was a fine actress and she could, and did, become a young girl or starving hag in front of our eyes; more probably, she willed us to think she was one of these by sheer force of her concentration. A more recent personal impression is that of a well-known contemporary dancer who possesses no remarkably beautiful attributes, but who arrives at moments of breathtaking perfection by sheer hypnosis of herself and her audience. I am referring to this sort of quality when I urge teachers to believe in mystery!

The depths of young people are not readily apparent, and, when auditioning untrained children, it is an advantage to give a small mime scene to be enacted. Often the most nervous and shy children will forget their surroundings by identifying themselves 100 per cent with the story to be told. These are the interesting pupils who will later develop into interpretive artists, and who have a gift which should be carefully preserved during the long, arduous and technical training to which a dancer is subject. I believe this 'sense of theatre' can be stimulated and encouraged by generally broadening the basis of ballet training to include classes in drama, mime and gesture, so that through these young artists of the future we may eventually all be enriched.

12. Health

The importance of good health to a dancer cannot be overemphasized. Any defect in the functioning of the body is a lessening of the efficiency of the dancer's instrument and, consequently, the ability to perform at top level. This is recognized in most athletes, who have to train for long periods in order to be in peak form for a particular race or competition; but it is not so generally understood that a dancer, in performance and rehearsal, uses supreme physical effort day after day and is expected, as an artist, to be consistently in control of technical feats requiring strength, endurance and vitality. The long training of dancers is a method of insuring against injury, but, while technique is a means of learning how to conserve strength and use of the body in the most intelligent and economical way, it can never supplant physical energy.

There are many cases of sickly children benefiting from learning dancing, as opposed to the old idea of good hard healthy outdoor sport. Pavlova, who was first turned down by the Maryinsky School as too weak and underdeveloped to embark on a career which would make such extreme demands upon her, must be the most celebrated example. However, the special nature of a dancer's constitution is found often in the brittle and nervous child rather than in one with a more robust physique, who, on reaching maturity, may coarsen and become unaesthetic.

Perhaps this chapter should be divided into two parts—mental and physical health—but, as research has proved, the two are indivisible, and in a dancer, especially so. The high degree of dependence upon a feeling of physical well-being makes a dancer abnormally conscious of small aches and pains, which, because a serious cause of the discomfort is feared, assume excessive importance and lead to over-dramatization of the ailment or even hypochondria, which is in the realm of mental health. However, with experience and professional work, most dancers learn to recognize the difference between real illness and nervous symptoms and also how to overcome small ailments by the spirit of performance or the regular discipline of a daily class; but the necessity for psychological health is certainly no less than that of the metabolism. This is a vast subject—but, though of particular interest and importance to teachers, one beyond the scope of this book.

Before a child is accepted in a school for serious classical ballet, the bone structure, and health of lungs and heart should be examined by a doctor. Also very important is the ability to rotate the leg outwardly in the hip joint. This must be more than 60 per cent if the boy or girl is to pursue a successful career as a classical dancer. During these examinations the proportions of limbs and tendons should be noted in relation to each other, as, if they are not properly harmonious, overdevelopment of muscles can ensue. The character of a child also plays a large part. Often a physically weak pupil, with the help of natural talent, enthusiasm, determination or a little of each, will develop into a strong dancer.

The main rules to follow are all dictated by common sense and should apply to the normal care and upbringing of every child: fresh air, regular but not excessive exercise, a balanced diet of wholesome food, and sufficient sleep. The time of puberty and early teenage often brings problems for children learning dancing. During these years too much is sometimes expected of a pupil. In academic lessons it is the time of examination and proof of future promise; in the ballet school it is the time when advanced work must be started. However, normally healthy girls should not have

trouble with menstruation if the regular amount of dancing activity is continued without extra strain. Often the exercise will be beneficial. Students should not, of course, be forced to work at these times if they feel really unwell, but it is not good to let a young person imagine herself to be 'sick' during the days of her period, as it is a total misunderstanding of the natural function of the body. If the periods are very irregular, medical guidance should be sought, but the taking of hormones should be avoided if possible as this can cause girls with certain constitutions to gain excessive weight and suffer from depression.

With both sexes the developing signs of maturity make children particularly sensitive and vulnerable, and overstrain should be carefully avoided.

Another real danger to dancers is dieting. Girls in their late teens often put on weight, and, when this is combatted by a self-inflicted semi-starvation diet, real physical and psychological damage can take place. Medical advice on dieting should be followed, and, where all the signs point to the natural state of the dancer being 'well-covered', he, or usually she, should be advised to embark upon another career lest too many of the precious training years before the age of twenty are wasted. Normal 'puppy fat' is not too serious and usually disappears if a child takes care not to indulge in cakes, sweets, chocolates and fatty foods.

Many dancers manage to have children without giving up their careers and childbirth is generally no more complicated for dancers than for other women. Whether or not the career is resumed afterwards often depends more on the practical state of affairs in the home in regard to domestic help and babysitting than on the mother regaining her figure. In general, women who have been dancers retain more zest for life and, very important, a good carriage, which is one of the best insurances against the illnesses of old age. Dancers, and especially dancing teachers, are renowned for long life and one is tempted to wonder if this is not because the arduousness of teaching is only endured by the superhumanly fit, rather than because the occupation itself is beneficial to the heart. Whichever explanation one inclines to accept, the fact remains that most dancers are healthy.

Many professionals in ballet companies come to believe that the regular daily class is essential for their well-being. During the period of rehearsing and performing this is, of course, absolutely true, but I believe times of complete rest are also necessary. Muscles and ligaments do become overworked and function less efficiently unless time is allowed for their recovery. It is also usually during periods of over-tension that injuries occur; therefore dancers must allow their bodies periodic respite, and they will find that after 'getting back into practice' nothing has been lost. If the rest is enforced, for example, following an injury after which a dancer cannot work for say three months, it should be reckoned that another three months training will be needed before the dancer reaches full strength again. This can be difficult to explain to commercial managers, or even to overworked and worried choreographers; but unless there is a wish to risk a recurrence of the injury, the slow 'come-back' should be observed. So often a pain or weakness becomes chronic because dancers are too impatient to start work again, and this is where a specialist should be consulted in order to decide whether the ambitions of a dancer should be temporarily curbed, or whether the fear and discomfort usually following an accident should be disregarded.

Massage is very good for relaxing taut muscles, and most dancers make use of it. It should be considered a prevention rather than cure and can be damaging to an

injury. In this case medical advice should be followed and at all times only a qualified masseur should be visited.

The care of the feet plays a vital role in the health of a dancer. Even small troubles such as corns and blisters can be so painful that a dancer will start to lift the shoulders or try to work without weight on one leg, simply to reduce the discomfort. This immediately brings bad habits into technique. Obviously it is again better to prevent the ailment by a little extra care. Not only should feet be kept scrupulously clean and dry, but also tights, socks and stockings must be washed frequently. Occasionally dancers pick up a painful infection commonly known as 'athlete's foot'. It can be caused by not sufficiently drying between the toes, but it is also contagious, and the bacteria can exist quite long and flourish in shoes or other contaminated pieces of wearing apparel, or equally well on the floor of showers. There are many pharmaceutical remedies, but it should be treated promptly, as cracks between the toes or other telltale signs will lead to further infection. Blisters can be avoided by not washing the feet immediately before dancing in point shoes, for this softens the skin and if the shoes are too hard and inflexible or even too large so that the foot has room to rub up and down inside, a sore place will inevitably occur. The knuckles of the toes, when rubbed with spirit, will grow a harder layer of skin, and it is advisable for dancers to do this regularly. Toenails should not be too long, and they should be cut to the shape of the toe in order to prevent in-growing. In general, girls and boys should wear heeled shoes when not dancing, in order to rest the Achilles tendon. This theory is not accepted by all specialists on the subject, and one must admit that primitive peoples, spending their lives barefoot, probably do not have trouble with their Achilles tendons, but then they are not expected either to rise on point or to complete a man's classical variation, full of steps of elevation. On the other hand, it is possible that civilized women constantly wearing high heels will, after a number of years, shorten the tendons behind their ankles; but surely dancers with so much daily work in flat shoes do not run this risk and need the slimming and relaxing effect of a heeled shoe when they are not dancing.

One great advantage dancers have is the ability to sweat healthily. Nervous perspiration under the armpits, which can smell so unpleasant, is not usual with dancers, nor do they suffer from the too-rapid perspiring of untrained bodies making uncustomary vigorous exertions. Rather, the whole body will sweat naturally, regulating the temperature and giving the dancer a supple feeling conducive to work.

Care must be taken after strenuous exercise that dancers do not get chilled. Wet practice clothes should be changed immediately, and, however warm dancers may be, they should not sit in draughts. Many professionals prefer to work in Mediterranean countries because warm air and a dry climate are far more pleasant, but strangely enough I find that 'mañana' lands (or should one say those where a siesta is essential?) have not produced nearly as many famous dancers as the European and North American continents. This is obviously a fairly wild generalization, and though I agree that damp climates are bad for dancers, it seems to me true that cold climates breed more energetic ones.

This chapter is intended to show dancers and teachers that health is often only a matter of common sense and good habits. All real illnesses and injuries should be treated by qualified medical practitioners, but these overworked mortals could be spared a little if only dancers would actively work to prevent accidents and ill health, and if any advice I have given here will enable them to do this, this short chapter will have served its purpose.

13. Rhythm and Musicality

Music, according to one dictionary, is 'the art of combining vocal and instrumental tones in a rhythmic form for the expression of emotion under the laws of beauty.' Surely the latter part of this definition applies directly to dancing, and, contrary to the belief of some musicians, music does play a very large part in the life of a dancer. It is therefore deplorable that in many ballet schools musical education is so abysmally neglected. Students freshly graduating into ballet companies—young, beautiful, ambitious and possessing strong and clean technique—find themselves ignored by choreographers if their rhythmic sense is weak, or if they cannot quickly grasp the complexities of phrase in contemporary music. In the *corps de ballet,* for example, a girl or boy out of time with the other dancers is absolutely useless, and as soloist the unmusical dancer (surely a contradiction in terms) will always remain second-rate. True musicality is both rhythmic and aural, but these two senses are not always equally present in one individual. A gross generalization, but one containing some truth, would be to place dancers in a group predisposed to rhythmic responses and instrumental players in an aural compartment. This is of course because the sensuality of music is expressed directly through the dancer's body, which is trained to do this, whereas the musician's approach to sound, though it may be emotional, is more analytical than that of a dancer and perhaps more direct. Obviously the possession of both perceptions lies in many artists, but a great danger arises when, for example, an instinctive rhythmic talent is mistaken for complete musicality, and cultivating the understanding of music is neglected. This is equally to be deplored in reverse.

It is interesting to observe that when music is syncopated, 90 per cent of people, dancers or not, will supply the missing beat by some movement of the body. Therefore, given a rhythm, it is a natural human characteristic to respond physically.

The 'anatomical' control of rhythm, conscious or unconscious, is generated in the knees, solar plexus and lungs, or so one must believe if one observes the primitive dances of African tribes and the current jigging in dancehalls and discothèques.

Any jumping up and down to music must use the knee joints as a speed control, and I wish more classical dancers would realize that their *demi plié* should also be used as an unconscious rhythm-giver! The lower centre of the torso generates most compulsive body movements, but due to the extreme discipline of the stomach and back in classical work, it is often one of the first natural sources of rhythm to be strangled by serious ballet training. Somehow a compromise has to be found, and I believe it is helpful to lift the 'dancing from the guts' feeling (never too bad a fault) to a point just under the breastbone. By doing this, the waist, instead of participating willy nilly in the movement of the hips, can take over more serious work, helping to strengthen the torso and connect the ribs and pelvis when necessary.

In the previous paragraphs I have had a simple repeated rhythm in mind which could be termed 'keeping the beat', but phrasing is also rhythm and has a shape of its own. Here breathing plays a very important part, and literally 'colours' the rhythmic movements a dancer makes. Much as a singer learns to control the voice by breath, so a dancer can govern the dynamics of motion by sharp intakes of breath or slow inhalations and exhalations. Of course most dance movements should have a musical compulsion, but too great awareness or analysis of·this can destroy a dancer's spontaneity in performance. It can bring a dangerous intellectual aridity into movement; an instinctive sense of when to fill the lungs is far better.

Breathing of course plays a larger part than this in dancing; one needs only to mention, as an obvious example, the athlete's preoccupation with the inhalation of sufficient oxygen in order to run faster, but we are here concerned with music, and it is enough to say that the respiration of dancers should be a bridge between the emotional and the physical response to sound.

Just as different species of animals have body rhythms appropriate to their size and their predatory and defence mechanisms, so men also have differing individual natural rhythm, usually established through a mixture of physique and character. This is easy to observe in dancers and becomes more pronounced as steps get more difficult and strenuous. A truly rhythmic dancer will use the spontaneous response of the body to music as a means of overcoming physical disadvantages. If, however, it is seen that the rhythmic sense of a student is not strong enough for him to make these adjustments subconsciously, a teacher should help him to achieve body speeds not natural to him by insisting upon all steps, and especially technical tricks and stunts, being executed at different tempi from that which is 'comfortable' to each individual. This is important, as later on it will distinguish between the dancer as circus performer and the dancer as musical interpretive artist. An *enchaînement* for advanced students, illustrating how the same steps can be executed in a sharp 2/4 or broad 3/4, is given later in the chapter.

The theory of music and the reading of scores should be mastered by dancers and are essential for anyone aspiring to choreography, the creative pinnacle of ballet. The choreographer stands alone and exposed, his work at the mercy of its interpreters, and the results at the mercy of critics. The 'idea', the seed which gives birth, must survive all the pitfalls of translation to a company of dancers. It must survive all the possible perils of faulty costume design, bad lighting, lack of time, money, or collaboration, and with reference to the subject of this chapter, the dangers of strange conductors, the shock of instrumental sound after rehearsing to a piano, and the inevitable discrepancy of tempi, due to insufficient combined stage and orchestra rehearsals.

Many young would-be choreographers fail, either for want of sufficient musical knowledge, or by boldly 'using' music whose complexities elude them. Of all highly specialized and skilled creative occupations, surely dance composition is the one most often abused by amateurs and dilettants. The most experienced choreographers will collaborate with composers and seek guidance from conductors, but a novice choreographer attempting his first ballet will probably not have this help, therefore a more solid musical background than is usually given whilst training dancers is almost essential if he is to survive the initial plunge. This lack of musical education could, more than is generally recognized, be the major dominating cause of the scarcity of choreographers.

Another attribute of dancers should be respect for the conductor. They should remember they will probably be dancing to a large orchestra, composed of musicians with technical and performing difficulties of their own, all of whom will be controlled by this individual. It is clear therefore that a working partnership, beginning in the studio, will produce the best results. All dancers know the agony of performing to unsympathetic tempi or combatting the non-understanding of movement displayed by some musicians, but previous discussion, cooperation and mutual respect will often prevent stormy stage rehearsals and smooth the path towards a real marriage of music and dance.

The difficulties of engaging a pianist ready and willing to play for classes cannot be ignored, but I would strongly advise teachers to keep up the search rather than 'make do' with a tape recorder. Apart from the tedious repetition, a mechanical accompaniment can never be a substitute for live music. I feel that even a mediocre pianist is better than a recording, though it is true that a bad accompanist can ruin a class. In many cases it is a matter of experience, and, with patience and help, a diffident or modest musician can be turned into an excellent and sympathetic pianist for class. If he or she prefers to improvise, the teacher must very clearly state the type of music required, give the tempo, and if possible demonstrate the steps whilst humming a tune. Should the pianist prefer to read music, plenty of books should be provided (there are many excellent collections of 'Music for Ballet Classes' on the market) with explanations of which pieces should be used and when. Usually after a few weeks a pianist will understand what is wanted and will also be able to give the necessary bars of introduction which should precede every *enchaînement* and which are so important to the dancer who understands how to use them as an indication of the tempi to follow.

I find in advanced classes it is occasionally advisable to give *enchaînements* in bars of 5/4 or 7/8 as later on dancers often have difficulties with irregular beats, and these rhythms are not complicated if one is slowly accustomed to them.

A simple exercise in 5/4 to be practised at the *barre* is:

1. *Battement frappé à la seconde,* with *fondu.*
2. Return *sur le cou de pied* and straighten supporting leg.
3.4.5. Repeat the two movements 1½ times.
1. Now bring the working foot *sur le cou de pied* and remain *en fondu.*
2. *Frappé à la seconde* straightening supporting leg.
3.4.5. Repeat the two movements 1½ times.
Repeat the whole combination 7 times. This can also be done with *relevé* and with double *frappé* (difficult). Teachers will find that many pupils have great trouble with this step if it is new to them, but that after several days it will no longer bother them.

Another exercise, which can be described as a 'trick' *enchaînement*, is executed to a mazurka. The feet follow the musical bars:

1. *Echappé sauté à la seconde.*
2. *Sauté* in this position.
3. *Fermée sauté en cinquième.*
   (Repeat 7 times)

The arms have a repeated sequence which takes 4 beats, and overlaps the rhythm of the feet:

1. Arms *cinquième en avant.*
2. Take the arms to *cinquième en haut.*
3. Bring the arms down *à la seconde.*
4. Finish in the commencing position, *en bas.*
   (Repeat 5 times)

Variations of this type of coordination exercise can be devised incorporating many further degrees of complexity.

The following *enchaînement* should be practised to a sharp 2/4 allegro and, in order to control different body speeds, to a broad 3/4 waltz tempo.

2/4 Time	3/4 Time	
and 1 and 2	(..3, 123,2)	*Temps de cuisse dessus* (hold working leg for a short moment in the *cou de pied* position)
and 3	(.23,3)	*Sissonne ouvert*, ending with *chassé passé croisé.*
and 4	(.23,4)	*Brisé dessus*, ending with the working leg *sur le cou de pied derrière.*
and er 5	(.23,5)	*Pas de bourrée dessous en tournant.*
and 6	(.23,6)	*Petit sissonne devant en tournant dehors.* Arms *cinquième en haut.*
and 7	(.23,7)	*Ballonné de côté*, ending with the working leg *sur le cou de pied derrière.*
and er 8	(.23,8..)	*Pas de bourrée dessous.*

Students should also regularly be asked during classes to give the time-signature of the music to which they are dancing, and, if possible, state what music it is, and who wrote it. This gives children the idea that it is important to know, and the habit of finding out should remain with them all through their professional careers. Most children have a definite propensity for learning and gain confidence when their environment, in this case the activities of the studio, is understood. If it is accepted that people's bodies generate tensions when confronted by the unknown, why should music be an exception? And if it is not an exception, then surely by acquainting children with facts about the sounds they hear and giving them countable accents with which they can physically identify, the teacher will help the timid or supposedly unmusical pupils to relax in their ballet classes.

Music classes in schools should not be purely theoretical but should also open a student's ears to the great richness of music perhaps not likely to be heard in the repertoire of ballet companies. Listening to concerts, radio and records must be encouraged, and the 'making' of music even more strongly so. Children learning to play the piano, violin or any other instrument can fairly easily be grouped together and supplemented by other students playing percussion instruments to form a small orchestra. What the result, to the fastidious ear, may lack in subtlety, is easily compensated for by the fervour of the participants. Making music together is, after all, very similar to dancing in a *corps de ballet,* where the dancer 'out of line' or 'not with the music' is equally as disturbing as the 'out of tune or tempo' orchestral player.

In fact nothing should be left undone that could enrich a dancer as an artist. Dancing is music made visible, song made tangible. Though transient in performance it is enduring as Art.

14. Pas de Deux

Pas de deux should be seen and not written about.

It is also better to practise one than to read about it, for the *pas de deux* speaks for itself. In the last fifty years classical ballet has developed technically and acrobatically at a giddy speed, but of all advances made *pas de deux* is the most striking. So many choreographers near the sublime when creating in this form that I believe—in schools especially—it should be approached with maximum respect. Not only is it the vehicle in which leading dancers climax their performance, but the breathtaking lifts and turns demanded by contemporary choreography are downright dangerous for inexperienced students.

A man and a woman dancing together, being after all what 'life' is about, provide limitless emotional opportunities. It is undoubtedly sensual, even in its most refined and abstracted form, and dancers with a physical awareness of each other will always dance better together than those lacking eroticism. This can be quite subconscious and in fact is usually preferably so because, although dancing glorifies the body, ballet is more esoteric than sexy.

It is possible for solo artists, always performing alone, to remain enclosed within the confines of self-expression and their own relation to external objects and compulsions. Is this why they sometimes fail to achieve greatness? They can express the ecstasies of joy, sorrow, pain and purity, but the mystic world of communion, other than with their muse which is a personal spiritual experience, or with the audience which is the normal desire of every performer, is not open to them. (One should not of course exclude communion with music, but this is again personal and more interpretive than creative in the case of performers.) A solo figure on an empty stage will arouse a given emotion in an audience, each member of which will usually identify with him, according to the illusions created by light, music and position, but if another figure is introduced, tension is immediately present and the emotion is dramatized. It is now possible to say 'anything can happen,' and this is surely fertile ground for choreographers.

Even a cursory examination of the well-known ballets leaves one in no doubt of where the dramatic climaxes lie and where inspired choreography is most often to be found: in the *pas de deux*.

The formal structure of a *pas de deux classique* comprises: *entrée, pas de deux*, boy's variation, girl's variation and coda. This form, perhaps best illustrated in the Petipa ballets, is still used by choreographers today, either in neoclassic one-act works or, as it was originally in the nineteenth century three-act narrative ballets, as a ceremonial dance for the hero and heroine. In these spectacular productions a *pas de deux* was often loosely interpolated into the plot to display second soloists. Both these divertissements and the *grand pas de deux* are now frequently to be seen taken out of their proper setting and performed by guest artists at charity matinees or the smallest hint of a Gala. As a means of indulging in a few bravura pyrotechnics it seems to me a regrettable practice, for the original intention of these dances is lost and only the tricks remain.

I think nearly all *grands pas de deux classiques* have greater excitement and can be better appreciated in their proper context. Fortunately those settings we still know are well preserved in the established companies, and due to their popularity with the general public, these museum-piece ballets seem unlikely to be put on the shelf for some years. Because they are strong in traditional discipline and techni-

cally allow no cheating, they are unique in their ability to mould dancers into soloists. That is why, in order to keep these ballets fresh, they are frequently refurbished with new productions, new sets, new 'approaches' and even new choreography, but usually the *pas de deux* remains sacrosanct.

In contemporary ballet the structural skeleton of these dances—the inherited bones—often remain. They have however became invisible to the undiscerning eye in a similar way to that in which graphic art has, to all outward appearances, discarded conventional perspective and proportion. This is necessary for ballet in order to penetrate beyond the visual into the subconscious, and I believe it is only possible because it is an art strong in its hereditary traditions. Voltaire said 'Dancing is an Art because it is subject to rules.' It is still possible to discern the truth of this in some of the most avant-garde and seemingly chaotic ballets of today, for when an ordered structure is present, however difficult to detect, the work is raised from the contemporary spawning of 'non-ballets' and 'dance happenings' to be worthy of reflection, analysis, and perhaps admiration.

The greatest good fortune to befall a young dancer is to begin his or her *corps de ballet* years in a company where exciting soloists are a day to day working example. I must stress 'day to day' because occasional exposure to famous guest artists is no substitute for the lessons to be learnt from regular observation of the costs of greatness. Probably in no other profession does success depend more upon hard work and talent and less upon luck. By absorbing the manner in which great *pas de deux* are created, rehearsed and performed, young dancers can prepare for the day when they are themselves the protagonists in these exciting working hours.

Let us examine these preparations for *pas de deux*. The technicalities of two people working together are not much more than the application of academic rules for classical ballet combined with consideration and respect for the partner.

It is a good idea for the girl to develop a sensitivity in the back of her head, so that she can maintain a tender relationship with her cavalier when standing in front of him. It is not necessary for her to look at him, she has only to think of him and incline her head for beautiful lines and the right quality to ensue. This harmony is essential to both dancers, and is usually most successful when instinctive and subconscious. The dancers must not contrive their partnership but let the lines result naturally from their shared emotions and rhythm. Mutual respect cannot be learned too soon; from the first class, girls must understand they are not yet ballerinas, but largely dependent upon their partners. Whereas the boys in their turn should not become semi-obscured lifting machines but develop manners both possessive and galant.

Brute strength is neither necessary nor attractive, for nearly all lifts are a co-ordination of effort and timing between the dancers. The man must be constantly aware of how the girl's weight is placed, the significant spot lying in the base of the spine. If, when she is standing on one leg, her balance is not directly over the supporting toe, she should remain rigidly in one piece, as her partner can then better judge which way she is falling and shift her back on to balance more directly. Girls with insufficient technique or an inclination to 'give' in the waist or pelvis should not be allowed to start *pas de deux* until the fault is corrected. This is especially important if inexperienced men or growing boys are learning to partner. Because in an average school in the West, male pupils are often fewer than girls, they are sometimes pre-

maturely pressed into *pas de deux* classes. The results of this impatience may not be noticed until several years later, when it is found that a man cannot sustain a three-act ballet with difficult partnering because of an earlier, and often undetected, spinal injury suffered when he was a boy.

At the beginning of the first class a boy should be asked how much taller he thinks his allotted partner will be when on point. He should then place his hands around an imaginary waist and the girl should walk on point into the circle to prove if he has gauged it correctly. Now let her make several *relevés* in the first position, while the boy learns how much adjustment is necessary to remain with his hands encircling her waist, both while she is in *demi plié* and while *sur les pointes*. After this, the girl should make a *relevé devant*, remaining completely controlled in one line from her toe to the top of the head, while the boy pushes her with his hands, either on her hip bones or her rib cage, from side to side, and forwards and backwards. This is a good preliminary for beginners, as it teaches the boy how much strength is required to put a girl back on her perpendicular balance after, for example, a faulty pirouette, and the girl learns to have confidence in the help she will receive and to avoid adjusting her own weight by wriggling about.

The next balance to be learnt must be well prepared by the girl in the following manner: standing *en cinquième sur les pointes* with one hand on the *barre,* she should make a high *développé devant,* sustain the lifted leg, and bring both arms to *cinquième en haut* for a short balance. Repeat the *développé* and balance in all positions *en croix*. It is very important that the pelvis should remain perfectly placed and well pulled up off the supporting leg. When sufficient strength and control has been built up this should be practised with a partner, the boy lightly holding one hand, or the girl's waist. His grip should be only nominal so that the girl learns to place herself on balance and so save her partner unnecessary extra work.

The correct distance between the dancers varies with the steps and the height of the individuals. Usually to be at arms length from each other is too far away, as there should be a certain play in the elbows, allowing the hands to move in and out as the balance requires. If the girl is tall for her partner it is sometimes necessary for the man to hold her wrists when standing behind her. A good dancer, of course, places herself on balance with the preliminary *piqué* or *relevé,* but should she subsequently lose her equilibre, she should never try to refind it alone. Often a dancer will lean forward in order to bring the weight forward, and of course this has the reverse effect, allowing the hips, in other words, the weight, to fall backwards.

A man should remain relaxed and at ease while supporting a girl, making sure that his partner is comfortable and, as often as possible, supporting herself. He should stand solidly on two feet but, for the sake of elegance, disguising the position to give the appearance of one relaxed leg.

There is a subtle difference between the manner in which an entrance is made before a *pas de deux* and the way in which one exits. It is easy to say that if 'good manners' are observed, all will fall correctly and instinctively into place, but in fact walking, running and especially the taking of curtain calls, need to be taught and practised; though in these things especially, young dancers tend to copy the stars they admire, sometimes excelling themselves in the speed with which they adopt mannerisms and affectations.

The teaching of conventional *pas de deux* from well known ballets is not necessary in the first year (quite apart from the pain it may cause anyone unfortunate enough to be watching), but I do think it important that from the beginning pupils should experience together broad movements travelling the length and breadth of the studio. In order therefore to prevent a class becoming too static, it is a good idea to let the dancers circle the room in pairs with fast moving mazurka or waltz steps. The latter, performed on a diagonal, with the boy behind the girl, making one half turn on every bar, is excellent and reveals very quickly how rhythmic a pupil is and how gifted in his or her ability to adapt to the shapes made by another person. *Pas de deux* is, after all, 'steps for two'.

A very real problem nowadays is how to prevent men from becoming too muscular in the shoulders. Contemporary *pas de deux* has become so complicated and the lifts so much more strenuous and 'perilous', there is a real danger that a strong dancer in the physical sense will be used for lifting to such an extent that the muscles around the neck will enlarge and stiffen, hampering the ease of his own solo work. If the warning signs are recognized in time, precautions can be taken to prevent this from happening, and the dancer can remain both strong and supple, which is essential for first soloists.

John Cranko was particularly brilliant at devising, and making work, lifts that should rightly be termed impossible. Although the strength for these feats is often shared by the girl and her partner and by co-ordinating the use of the spine and *plié,* I found it beneficial to give daily shoulder limbering exercises in the Stuttgart boys' classes to counteract any tendency towards over-muscular shoulders. It is useless to go on asking a boy with high, knotted shoulders to pull them down. The very act of doing this brings muscles into play which cause a rigidity. It is far better to limber and relax the tension, so that the shoulders will 'fall away' from the ears.

Boys should be prepared for 'lifts' by special exercises to strengthen the arms and spine. 'Push-ups' as performed by an athlete lying prone face down, the hands palm downwards on the ground by his shoulders, are an effective preparation. Also beneficial is for a boy to hang from a bar by his hands, his body fully stretched; then, without pause, make as many arm bends as possible, each time bringing his chin above the level of the bar.

When lifting, boys should endeavour to get below the weight of the girl at the same time as she makes her preparatory *plié.* The weight can then be taken in the boy's thighs, as he lifts the girl before stretching his knees. Without this good *plié* a man will lean forward to get a grip on a girl's waist, and, as he takes her weight, the resulting strain on his back can be damaging to the spine. Experienced men will sometimes time this *plié* to slightly follow that of the girl, thereby using her push off to facilitate coming beneath her. Getting under the weight of the girl entails moving forward a little when she is in the air. To pull her backwards, if the lift is from the waist, force her to 'break' in the middle and her legs will come forward. When the girl makes her preparatory *plié* before springing, she should be careful not to 'sit out' at the back or to let her shoulders fall forward. Both actions prevent her partner from getting close enough to add his strength to the take-off, and the subsequent straightening of the girl is often jerky and unattractive.

A boy, when starting to learn how to lift, will often not realize that it is the placing of his partner on the floor after holding her aloft that is the most difficult and important part. He will use all his strength to push his girl into the air, hold her there

as long as possible, and then be too exhausted to control her coming down. It is, after all, the gentle descent and soundlessness of the ballerina, which give an illusion of ease. This also requires the most strength from both dancers. For the girl it can be most distressing to be held in the air too long, and results in several faults, two of which are as follows. If the girl's supporting foot does not reach the ground before the rhythmic beat dividing the springs, the girl will have no time to *plié* and the lifts will become unmusical and without co-ordination. Secondly, many lifts, such as a simple *grand jeté en avant,* have a definite parabolic shape; if this is interrupted by the boy sustaining his partner too long in one position, the girl will lose her curve through the air and start to 'hang'. This can be minimized, but not indefinitely, if the girl uses her stomach and back muscles with the correct tension, but it is more often the boy's error. It is of course easier for him to support the girl when his arms are fully stretched beneath her, but postponing the strenuous descent is a sign of weakness.

Regular *enchaînements* for building strength slowly and surely, in order to perfect this deceptive quality of ease, should be given from the first *pas de deux* class and are simple to understand.

A sequence of steps containing *glissades, jetés, assemblés, changements,* or more advanced steps of *petit sauts* suitable for performing alone, should be arranged. The girl must then execute this, using her own elevation and strength. Now, very slightly slower, this same sequence should be performed with the boy supporting the girl on the waist but making sure that the rhythm is not disturbed by suspending her too long in the air. As the months progress, the speed should be reduced until both dancers have sufficient strength to perform the *enchaînement* as though in slow motion and with no signs of strain.

In general it is combined tactics that achieve the best results, and I can only recommend that both dancers make efforts to ensure that their partners want to dance with them. How tiresome it is when each dancer is full of complaints about the performance of the other. How often one hears the girl demanding 'push me here,' and 'lift me there,' until her partner is reduced to the role of bulldozer or crane. It should be a matter of personal pride to all dancers that they are desirable as partners.

Here are three preliminary exercises for students starting *pas de deux* classes:

The boy stands directly behind the girl, his hands on her hip bones. The girl does 4 *echappés,* (3/4 time, one *echappé* to each bar). The boy meanwhile gauging exactly how much higher her waist is going to be when she is on point and how much lower when *en fondu.*

The girl then makes a *relevé devant* and holds for 4 bars, on the last beat closing the working foot *derrière* in fifth.

This is repeated until the boy can immediately 'feel' her balance on the *relevé* and keep her weight over the working foot, should she sway in any direction.

The exercise is then repeated, the girl making two *echappés,* and the *relevé* earlier. (She must fold her arms on her chest and ensure that the working knee is not too high, nor the hip lifted.) On the last four bars, the boy turns the girl once by giving a small sharp pull towards him on the hip bone of her working

leg side, and at the same time a push with the base of the palm behind the hip bone on the other side.

He will soon become accustomed to this low position of the hands, as it affords a firm, bony grip in direct relationship to the leg and is far better than on the waist, which is less defined and too supple. During an *en dehors* turn to the right, the man should have his left hand on the girl's waist, so that she revolves away from his fingertips, thereby avoiding the danger of their entanglement in any embroidery or loose material upon her costume. The right hand should be free for adjusting the balance, should it be necessary, and stopping the turn. The girl should *relevé* tidily into the turning position and maintain this throughout, whatever happens. In general, terrific impetus or a wild push off is fatal, as is 'scares' the man and simply achieves a solo pirouette with a supported finish only if the ballerina is lucky enough to have a hero as her partner.

Another similar exercise is to replace the *relevé* with a *changement*, the girl taking her arms to *cinquième en haut* and remaining very straight and upright in the body, the legs firmly held together and stretched in fifth.

Here the man must grip the girl very slightly above the waist in order to lift her from under the rib cage. He will find this easier if he presses the little finger edge of his hands towards each other and does not try to encircle the waist with first fingers and thumbs.

The lift must be perfectly co-ordinated by a mutual musical accent and a short sharp *plié* from the girl. The descent must be as slow as possible. If the boy allows some of the weight to fall on his chest, he must be careful not to pull the girl's waist too far backwards, or she will be unable to retain her straight line and will tilt the legs forward.

A third exercise can be made travelling on a diagonal. Five or six boys, according to the space available, are placed across the room from one corner to another, facing downstage corner and standing in a large fourth *ouverte* with the front knee bent and the weight over it, the arms extended sideways.

The girls follow one another travelling down the line.
To a slow count 4/4:
Glissade, piqué en arabesque ouverte (and 1)
(The girl places her upstage hand on the boy's downstage shoulder and her other on the hand or waist of his outstretched arm. She must be careful not to press on this hand but, when necessary, grip firmly on his shoulder, which is more solid.)
Hold this position (2,3,4)
The girl lets go her support and balances (5,)
The man steps back and behind her and steadies her arabesque by holding both hip bones (6,7.)
The girl makes a *chassé passé* (8.)
Now the boy returns to his original fourth position and the girl moves on to the next boy.

140

These three very simple exercises are good basic preparation for turns, lifts and balance, respectively.

Pas de deux is almost certainly the most enjoyable form of dancing. What else can explain so many folkdances being executed in pairs or the ballroom being the source of so many tender romances? Brought to the ultimate in the classical *pas de deux,* it is a fairly ecstatic feeling for a girl to be carried the width of a stage at arms length above a man's head.

All the technical impossibilities of the solo—slow motion jumping, non-ending pirouettes and the daydreams of students—are made reality in *pas de deux.* This may sound as if the girl has the best of it—and perhaps she has—but if the movements are properly shared by both partners, she should become the passive half, creating the shapes and spirals he decides. This has been wonderfully demonstrated in the great partnerships of the past: Irene and Vernon Castle, Ginger Rogers and Fred Astaire, Karsavina and Nijinsky, Markova and Dolin, to name but a few that spring to mind.

It appears therefore that to be successful, the dancers must have a relationship both physical and spiritual, and it does no harm to start off young aspirants with a proper awareness of this. Afterwards, music is the mediator which can save the contestants from battle and transform all into a *pas de deux* worthy to stand side by side with the great love duets of opera and classic theatre.

Conclusion

In spite of the technicalities contained in these chapters, it has not been my intention to provide a textbook. Rather, my aim has been to open the eyes of any students still riveted to the pursuit of technique to the wonder of other possibilities.

So often the mountain is obscured by minor peaks and young dancers wonder what they are really aiming for. Basking in the admiration of fellow students and the pride of teachers is encouraging and pleasant, but if the one turns to envy and the other to possessiveness, a dancer can feel life has suddenly been emptied of love.

It is true that ballet today has become extremely technical, conforming in this to our time and age, but it is an impoverished state of affairs if this is all it has to offer. By all means strive for a technical purity, for perfection is mathematics and mathematics is art bringing its own emotion; this is a lofty goal and along the way a few human failings do no harm. They can be lovable, they are sometimes fun, and would not dancers be a dreary, earth-bound lot if zest for life were missing?

For over a hundred and forty pages I have exhorted the foot to be stretched and the leg turned out, now my advice is to forget everything and just get out there and dance.